Micro-Reflection on Classroom Communication

Micro-Reflection on Classroom Communication
A FAB Framework

Hansun Zhang Waring and Sarah Chepkirui Creider

SHEFFIELD UK   BRISTOL CT

Published by Equinox Publishing Ltd.

UK: Office 415, The Workstation, 15 Paternoster Row, Sheffield,
        South Yorkshire S1 2BX
USA: ISD, 70 Enterprise Drive, Bristol, CT 06010

www.equinoxpub.com

First published 2021

British Library Cataloguing-in-Publication Data
A catalogue record for this book is available from the British Library.

ISBN-13   978 1 78179 735 8   (hardback)
          978 1 78179 736 5   (paperback)
          978 1 78179 737 2   (ePDF)

Library of Congress Cataloging-in-Publication Data
Names: Waring, Hansun Zhang, author. | Creider, Sarah Chepkirui, author.
Title: Micro-reflection on classroom communication : a FAB-framework /
  Hansun Zhang Waring and Sarah Chepkirui Creider, Teachers College,
  Columbia University.
Description: Sheffield, South Yorkshire ; Bristol, CT : Equinox Publishing
  LTD, 2021. | Series: Reflective practice in language education |
  Includes bibliographical references and index. | Summary: "Based on over
  a decade of fine-grained analysis of video-recorded ESL classroom
  interaction, this book offers a way of seeing and gauging the quality of
  classroom communication beyond distributions and categories. It invites
  reflective conversations on how three principles of skillful classroom
  communication - Fostering, Attending, and Balancing - may be practiced
  in the micro-moments of classroom interaction"-- Provided by publisher.
Identifiers: LCCN 2020027519 (print) | LCCN 2020027520 (ebook) | ISBN
  9781781797358 (hardback) | ISBN 9781781797365 (paperback) | ISBN
  9781781797372 (ebook)
Subjects: LCSH: Interaction analysis in education. | Reflective teaching. |
  Video tapes in education. | English language--Study and
  teaching--Foreign speakers.
Classification: LCC LB1034 .W36 2020 (print) | LCC LB1034 (ebook) | DDC
  371.102/4--dc23
LC record available at https://lccn.loc.gov/2020027519
LC ebook record available at https://lccn.loc.gov/2020027520

Typeset by S.J.I. Services, New Delhi, India

For our daughters

Contents

Editor's Preface   ix

Acknowledgments   xi

Chapter 1: Introduction   1

Chapter 2: Foster an Inviting Environment   18

Chapter 3: Attend to Learner Voices   60

Chapter 4: Balance Competing Demands   84

Chapter 5: The FAB Classroom: Bringing It All Together   111

Chapter 6: Conclusion   131

Appendix A: Transcription Notations   138

Appendix B: List of Extracts   140

References   142

Index   149

Editor's Preface

Hansun Waring and Sarah Creider's book, *Micro-Reflection on Classroom Communication: A FAB Framework*, encourages TESOL teachers to reflect on their teaching by examining the quality of classroom communications that take place during a language lesson. Based on over a decade of fine-grained analysis of video-recorded ESL classroom interaction, this book offers a very interesting way for inexperienced and experienced practicing teachers to 'see' and reflect on the quality of classroom communication beyond distributions and categories. In particular, by parsing detailed transcripts of actual classroom interaction, this excellent book invites reflective conversations on how three principles of skillful classroom communication may be practiced in the micro-moments of classroom interaction: (1) fostering an inviting classroom environment, (2) attending to student voices, and (3) balancing competing demands (FAB). Attention to the moment-by-moment complexity of the classroom also allows teachers to learn and practice the skill of noticing, the first step in an iterative cycle of noticing and changing. That is, along with reflecting on what *happened* in a classroom, teachers must also learn to notice what *is happening* in the moment. The goal of such an approach is to cultivate a mentality of micro-reflection—one that sensitizes teachers to the consequentiality of every move they make as they make them in the simultaneity and sequentiality of second-by-second classroom interaction.

Hansun Waring and Sarah Creider, two very experienced language educators working out of Columbia University, New York, have written a highly readable, engaging, and absorbing book that goes to the heart of the ESL classroom where both teachers and students engage in important communication that fosters language learning. After contextualizing and establishing the importance of what they call 'micro-reflection' on classroom communication, the opening chapter introduces readers to the theoretical principles as well as the empirical grounding underpinning the FAB framework for reflecting on classroom communication. Following this introduction are three chapters that focus on the three components of FAB and a fourth that brings them together in the classroom. Each chapter, while using a great variety of transcripts from actual classroom interaction that capture a full range of interactional details, includes a wealth of ideas, questions and activities, and reflections that spotlight previously unaddressed aspects of classroom communication that feature subtlety, richness, and a full range of complexities of teaching in its microscopic details. The chapters also offer a multimodal approach that emphasizes noticing and reflecting on all aspects of classroom communication, including not just talk, but also gesture and the physical environment, along with specific exercises to help students build the skill of noticing, as it relates to micro-reflection. The book ends with an argument for moving from micro-reflection towards a 'micro-revolution' of classroom interaction, suggesting that changing teacher-student dynamics and promoting student agency begins at the micro-level.

Pre-service and in-service language teachers, language teacher educators, and teachers and teacher educators beyond language education will find this a useful and enjoyable book that they can work through on their own or with a group of colleagues. *Micro-Reflection on Classroom Communication: A FAB Framework* brings reflection and interaction in the classroom together in a practical, theoretically-driven manner by focusing on micro-moments as a foundation for micro-reflection, and as such, gives language teachers concrete tools for noticing and reflection.

Thomas S. C. Farrell
Series Editor, *Reflective Practice in Language Education*

Acknowledgments

Hansun: After the 2016 publication of my *Theorizing Pedagogical Interaction: Insights from Conversation Analysis*—a milestone project for me in many ways, I kept toying with the idea of translating the many insights into actionable knowledge for teachers and teacher educators. Tom's invitation back in May 2017 gave me the perfect platform for this wish-list item, and with Tom being one of the most authentic, brilliant, and passionate TESOL teacher educators of our time, I couldn't think of a better visionary to shepherd this project. Still, I didn't quite have the gumption to make the dive. Notes were scribbled, and a proposal-like draft pieced together. It all felt utterly uninspiring, so I let it sit—until October that same year. As I was ending my book talk with the usual wish to go practical, I saw Sarah in the audience, and then and there, I finally saw a way to make my wish come true. For years, I have been a big fan of Sarah's ingenious mind, her splendid writing, and last but not least, her intoxicating humanity. I am so grateful that she said yes, and this book came into shape in the subsequent months over many coffees and lunches at Le Pain Quotidien and Caffe Reggio in the Greenwich Village of New York City. I would not be having the ideas I have and doing the writings I do without the rich intellectual soil that is the #lansibunch, of which Sarah is one of the originals. To all my doctoral students present and past, thank you for keeping me 'alive'—in more ways than you know—through our numerous, and often high-spirited and laughter-filled, conversations and data sessions. My now 11-year-old daughter Zoe is a daily reminder of all the amazing teachers that have given me the wonder of this child. Last but not least, to Michael, thank you for giving me the freedom to soar and a home that still is, and will always be, my safest, and favorite place to be.

Sarah: When Hansun asked if I would work with her on a book for teachers, designed to offer a micro-approach to reflective teaching, I was both honored and thrilled. Honored because of Hansun's brilliant research on pedagogical interaction, which is foundational for so many of us in this field. Thrilled because this project seemed to provide an avenue for working with a paradox that comes up again and again in my work with teachers. As conversation analysis teaches us, responding to what's happening right now—with this particular person and at this particular moment—is at the heart of human interactions. However, if this responsiveness is largely unconscious, teachers also need to make conscious choices about their words and gestures, based on their pedagogical goals. Staying aware of these choices while also staying present with the person in front of us is an incredibly important teaching skill. My own ability to handle this double-layered awareness has been radically shifted by studying conversation analysis. Not only does the field offer rich insights regarding the work of teachers and students, it also trains us in how to attend to the details of an interaction, as it unfolds. I am lucky enough to have been introduced to conversation analysis in a class taught by Hansun. I will always remember visiting her office during that semester, and watching her replay the same few seconds of a dinner-table conversation over and over again. She brought total skill and attention to one tiny pause, showing me both the importance of 6/10ths of a second of silence and—even more importantly—modeling how to approach close analysis of talk. My hope is that this book provides at least a taste of that experience for readers, and that it inspires an understanding of the importance and possibility of each tiny moment of interaction.

Tom's work on reflective teaching is also a longstanding source of inspiration, and it is a privilege to be part of this project, and to be in touch with such an amazing group of colleagues, all of whom approach teaching with respect and integrity. Similarly, the classroom teachers I work with—whether they are new to the field or bring decades of experience—provide companionship, rigor, and a reminder of the macro-issues I can lose sight of in my obsessions with pauses and prepositions. I'm also grateful to my own teacher-mentors, particularly Barbara Hruska and Annie Ellman. When I talk with students about the importance of finding mentors, I always mention that my own primary mentor is my mother, Peggy Reimann—who also happens to be a master teacher. Trying to understand and explain what she does so beautifully in her interactions with students is a big part of what led me into this field in the first place. On the other end of the family tree, my daughter Anna is a constant reminder of the joy that waits in the present moment, and her strong sense of justice pushes me to see both sides of every teacher-student interaction. Most of all, I am forever grateful to my husband Joe, who has supported every single one of my wild goals with the perfect combination of love, puns, amazing dinners, and philosophical conversations.

Chapter 1

Introduction

Reflection is an age-old topic in (language) teacher education. In this chapter, we begin with the rich body of literature addressed to reflective practices (RP) both conceptually and empirically. We note the overall 'macro' focus of this literature, which we hope to complement with an approach that we have come to call 'micro-reflection.' We briefly introduce what such micro-reflection entails and how conversation analysis (CA) makes it possible to document the details of pedagogical interaction that lie at the foundation of micro-reflection. We then present what we call the 'FAB' framework, as a tool for conceptualizing the 'content' of micro-reflection (i.e., what can be reflected upon as we engage in micro-reflection) and the transcription system for documenting the micro. The chapter ends with an overview of the book.

FROM MACRO TO MICRO

This section offers an overview of research on reflective practice for teachers in general, as well as a look at works with a specific focus on reflection and second-language teaching. We start with two seminal figures in the field of reflective teaching: John Dewey and Donald Schön. Next, we ask how reflection has been defined more recently, and what methods have been used for encouraging and facilitating reflection.

Seminal Theorists on Reflection

Educator John Dewey's book *How we think* (1910) is often considered a forerunner of current work on reflective teaching. For Dewey, reflection was the most valuable component of a carefully delineated typology of thinking, and the only form that that was 'truly educative in value' (p. 2). Like most researchers today, Dewey saw reflection as starting from a point of difficulty, or a 'problem' (p. 9).

However, noting the problem was only a first step. For true reflection to occur, Dewey called for 'systematic...inquiry' (p. 13), including an examination of the evidence that supported (or not) the thinker's underlying beliefs.

Over seventy years after the publication of *How we think*, Donald Schön's (1983) work *The reflective practictioner* extended and deepened Dewey's description of reflective thought. The idea that reflection might occur during action was one of Schön's important contributions to this field. Thus, for Schön, reflection moved beyond a logical exploration that occurs after a problematic situation has taken place, to also include the more intuitive ability to reflect as the situation is occurring. Notably, the author's description of how these complexities play out for teachers rings as true today as it did almost forty years ago, when his work was first published: 'Teachers are faced with pressures for increased efficiency in the context of contracting budgets, demands that they rigorously "teach the basics," exhortations to encourage creativity, build citizenship, help students to examine their values' (p. 17). For an in-depth appreciation of Dewey and Schön's legacy in laying the foundation for the literature on reflection and reflective practices, see Farrell (2019).

Definitions and Models of Reflection

Since the publication of Schön's work, interest in reflective teaching has grown. Indeed, many teacher education programs seem to treat the importance of reflection as a given (Beauchamp, 2015; Farrell, 2018a; McGarr & Moody, 2010; Walsh & Mann, 2015). Researchers working in second language teacher education (SLTE) have also focused on the importance of reflection (Brandt, 2008; Copland, Ma, & Mann, 2009; Farrell, 2018a). Despite the difficulty of defining reflection as well as the controversies surrounding its definition (Akbari, 2007; Beauchamp, 2015; Farrell, 2008, 2018b; Rodgers, 2002; Walsh & Mann, 2015), general education scholars have offered important insights into how reflection may be defined. For a cogent and comprehensive review of this question, see Farrell (2019), who also offers his own definition as a result of this review:

> A cognitive process accompanied by a set of attitudes in which teachers systematically collect data about their practice, and, while engaging in dialogue with others, use the data to make informed decisions about their practice both inside and outside the classroom. (Farrell, 2015, p. 123)

Rather than offering a definition, many authors conceptualize reflection as a model or framework that contains multiple levels. Often, the highest level is considered 'critical' (Hatton & Smith, 1995; see also Farrell, 2018a; Lawrence-Wilkes & Ashmore, 2014; and Sparks-Langer et al., 1990). Here, teachers move beyond simply noting their practice to reflecting on bigger-picture questions that may play themselves out in their teaching, related to societal or even moral issues. Farrell (2015) proposes five stages/levels to achieve a 'holistic reflective practice experience' as teachers become more aware of their *philosophy*, *principles*, *theory*, and *practice* and critically examine broader issues that impact their practice both inside and outside the classroom (pp. 22–23). As Farrell (2015) observes, teachers are able to create better opportunities for learning as a result of greater awareness of 'who they are, what they do, how they do it, and why they do it' (p. 33).

Methods and Content for Reflection

Just as there seems to be a lack of consensus regarding the definition of reflection, researchers have also described a great variety of methods for reflective teaching, as well as a range of topics considered worthy of reflection. One way of clarifying methods may be to think about when reflection takes places in relation to the events being reflected on. Most commonly, we think about reflection *on*, which would take place after teaching (Farrell, 2018b; Walsh & Mann, 2015). As we mention above, Schön (1983) built on Dewey (1910) in his description of how skilled practitioners can reflect *during*, or in the midst of action. More recently, scholars have also discussed reflection *for* (Farrell, 2008, 2018b; Grushka, McLeod, & Reynolds, 2005), or reflection that is part of the planning process for future events. We can also note that when reflection takes place is related to how it is accomplished. Most commonly, reflection has been conducted through journals and diaries (Walsh & Mann, 2015; Farrell, 2018a). However, some authors have suggested that reflection should take place in dialogue, and be a collaborative process (Beauchamp, 2015; Walsh & Mann, 2015; Liu, 2017; Saito & Khong, 2017).

Interestingly, given the proliferation of research on reflective teaching, there seems to be surprisingly little work explicitly focused on topics or content for reflection. Most writers follow Dewey's (1910) assumption that the first impetus for reflection is a perceived problem. There also seems to be a general consensus that reflection relates to broad issues such as teacher belief systems and teacher identity (Beauchamp, 2015; Farrell, 2008, 2018a, 2018b; Liu, 2015). At the same time, and perhaps particularly for language teachers, whose content is also the medium of instruction (Long, 1983), researchers have acknowledged a need to look specifically at communication within the classroom (Farrell, 2008, 2018b;

Walsh, 2011; Walsh & Mann, 2015). For instance, Walsh & Mann (2015), in their article calling for 'data-led' (p. 351) reflection, advocate the use of transcripts.

In sum, reflective teaching is often seen as starting from a specific problem encountered in practice. There seems to be a general acknowledgment of a lack of a clear definition of reflection, although many researchers offer a view of the process that is based on a series of levels, moving from more descriptive to more critical, or more abstract to more concrete. While the idea of reflection during (or before) action has been acknowledged in the literature, most case studies seem to describe reflection as being separate from practice. Finally, researchers have discussed the importance of interaction as topic of reflection, particularly for language teachers. However, descriptions of reflection-on-interaction remain relatively macro in scope. Even researchers who use transcripts seem to focus on identifying behavior with preconceived codes, rather than on a more bottom-up noticing of the fine details of interaction.

The *How* of Reflection

In a sense, the lack of consensus regarding a definition of reflection, while troubling if it leads to sloppy or careless practice, may also be a sign of a lively and rich field. Reflection is only interesting if it leads to change—and change can only occur within a system with room for multiple points of view. Thus, rather than describing a new definition or framework, our goal is to offer specificity in both methods and content. We suggest that detailed descriptions of how teachers can develop the skill of reflection and use that skill to affect change in practice is one missing piece in the field. Part of building that skill involves helping teachers develop the ability to notice (see also Mason, 2002). Rather than asking *How do you think it went?*, for example, we might probe with *What did Ana say when you said and did X?* In fact, from a conversation analytic (CA) perspective (see below), rather than start the reflective process with a perceived problem or issue, we engage in 'unmotivated looking' (Psathas, 1995), treating any given moment of interaction as containing important information. This may be one way to avoid the tendency for reflective practice to become 'ritualized' (Farrell, 2018a). As Hansen (2017) writes, 'reflective understanding' (p. 15) is the result of a receptive and engaged—but also open-minded—attentiveness. Thus, in this book, we use the tool of micro-reflection to help teachers notice the powerful choices that can be made in even the most apparently mundane moments (Jacknick & Creider, 2018) of teaching and learning. In our attention to the micro-level, however, we are not ignoring the importance of critical reflection, Instead, as we discuss in our final chapter, we believe that one way of moving towards a critical view of our roles and identities as teachers is to start in the moment-by-moment details of our work in the classroom. Thus, while big-picture, or 'macro' reflection is clearly important, we suggest that micro-reflection is also a crucial component of reflective language teaching. In fact, we believe such reflection to various degrees embodies Farrell's (2019) six principles of reflective practice (i.e., holistic, evidence-based, dialogic, bridging principles and practices, requiring an inquiring disposition, a way of life), heralding, in particular, a close-to-the-ground version of 'evidence-based.' Finally, we follow Schön's understanding of the skill required for reflection in action, but would add that such skill can be taught and learned. The development of this skill is at the heart of the cycle of micro-reflection, which we describe in the next section.

THE CYCLE OF MICRO-REFLECTION: NOTICING AND CHANGING

Many teachers are familiar with the sensation of looking back at a recently completed class or lesson and realizing that the entire experience has receded into a fuzzy memory. It is particularly difficult for novice teachers (or experienced teachers working in new settings, or with new materials) to be attentive enough during teaching to remember the experience in any detail. However, in order to reflect on the act of teaching, teachers need to build the skill of noticing themselves, their students, and their environment. And, clearly, there is no way for teachers to make careful, reflective choices in the classroom if they are not aware of the 'choice points' (Hepburn, Wilkinson, & Butler, 2014, p. 248) as these pivotal moments come up. To put it differently, we suggest that a missing link in the discussion of reflection is helping teachers to develop the ability of 'gathering data' (Walsh & Mann, 2015) for reflection by noticing their actions (and those of their students) in the moment.

The cycle of micro-reflection, then, starts with noticing (see 'experience' and 'description' as elements of reflection in Rodgers, 2006), with an in-the-moment

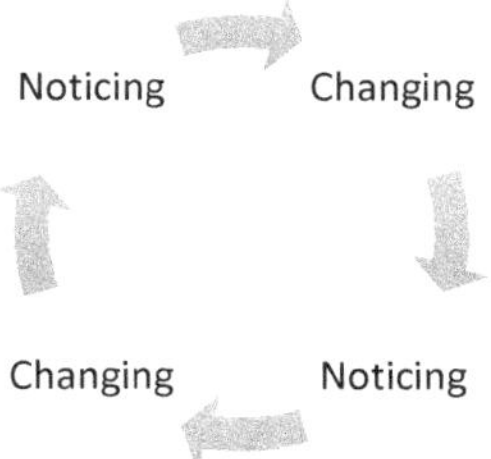

Figure The iterative cycle of micro-reflection

awareness of micro-details within the complex, multivocalic (Waring, 2016) world of the classroom. It is only after we notice—and, of course, reflect on what we have noticed—that we can begin to make changes in our practice. At this point, noticing is again necessary, as teachers bring their awareness to the specific factors they are focusing on, and thus the iterative cycle of reflection begins again. The figure above offers a visual of this cycle.

ACCESSING THE MICRO: CONVERSATION ANALYSIS (CA)

In this section, we introduce conversation analysis (CA) as an analytical tool for accessing the micro aspects for (classroom) interaction, remarking on its power as a catalyst for what we call micro-intervention.

CA as a Microscopic Tool

A time-tested tool for accessing micro-understandings of human interaction is conversation analysis (CA). Founded by sociologists Harvey Sacks, Emmanuel Schegloff, and Gail Jefferson in the late 1960s, conversation analysis is known as a form of 'naturalistic inquiry' into social interaction, distinct in its insistence on capturing 'conduct as it has been preserved in audio and video recordings' (Clayman & Gill, 2004, p. 590) as opposed to conduct as reported by the participants or obtained through field notes, native intuitions, or experimental methodologies (Heritage, 1984, p. 236). These audio and video recordings are then transcribed using notations originally developed by Gail Jefferson (Jefferson, 2004) and modified to accommodate multimodal conduct (see below) that indicate a full range of interactional details such as volume, pitch, pace, intonation, overlap, inbreath, smiley voice, length of silence, gaze directions, facial and hand gestures, body postures and movements, as well as features of the material surround. In this book, for the purpose of truly accessing the micro in our cycle of micro-reflection, we will be gradually familiarizing our readers with the CA transcription system. At the same time, for readability, we will also be simplifying portions of transcripts that might not be the focus of our explication.

Analysts work with audio or video recordings along with the transcripts to 'uncover the usually unconscious—but nonetheless extremely skillful—discourse analyses speakers perform as they interpret and respond to their fellow conversationalists, pause by-pause, word-by-word, gesture-by-gesture, and turn-by-turn' (Creider, 2014, p. 39). Analysis begins with a meticulous inspection of single instances that revolves around 'consistently and insistently' asking a single question

(Heritage & Clayman, 2010, p. 14): 'Why that now?' (Schegloff & Sacks, 1973), i.e., why a particular bit of talk is produced in that particular format at that particular time; what is it accomplishing? It is in these minute details that evidence is located for how social actions such as requesting or resisting are accomplished by the participants themselves. A two-year-old's *My legs are tired*, when said in a specific way at a specific time directed to a specific person with a specific ensemble of gaze, gesture, and body posture is hearable as a request (i.e., *Pick me up*), and it is indeed taken by the participants themselves as a request, as evidenced in the parent's subsequent move to pick the child up. For practitioners, an undisputable value of CA lies in its ability to access the 'high-definition' view of interaction and to unveil 'versions of interactional events which are markedly counter-intuitive' (McHoul, 1985, p. 57). After all, it is only by grasping the 'truth' of what actually happened in its full range of vivid details that productive reflections can be fostered and positive changes engineered.

CA for Micro-Intervention

For the past four decades, CA has been building a strong track record of yielding in-depth understandings of professional practices in a wide variety of contexts (e.g., Drew & Heritage, 1992), forming an important knowledge base upon which practitioners can draw to identify problems, devise solutions, and enhance efficacy (e.g., Antaki, 2011). CA findings have been utilized to improve aphasic conversations (Wilkinson, 2011), raise response rates in telephone interviews (Maynard, Schaeffer, & Freese, 2011), enhance the efficacy of telephone service deliveries (Drew et al., 2014; Hepburn, Wilkinson, & Butler, 2014; Sikveland & Stokoe, 2016), facilitate the diagnosis of neurological conditions (Jenkins & Reuber, 2014), inform the design of interaction spaces (Luff et al., 2014), gather more patient concerns (Heritage & Robinson, 2011), and even help politicians obtain applause during their speeches (Atkinson, 2015).

These CA-based interventions are what we would call 'micro-interventions,' as they target the small details of interactional behavior to generate incremental, and yet powerful changes. One way of obtaining applause, for example, is to build three-part lists (Atkinson, 2015); one way to gather more patient concerns is to substitute the word *some* for *any* in *Any questions?* (Heritage & Robinson, 2011), and one way to improve aphasic conversation is for the non-aphasic partner to withhold any initiations of repair and let 'errors' pass (Wilkinson, 2011). In all these cases, CA insights constitute the basis of micro-interventions, which would then involve iterative cycles of awareness-raising exercises targeting specific interactional behaviors along with thoughtful discussions of alternatives that may be employed at various 'choice points' of the interactions (Hepburn et al., 2014, p. 248).

An exemplary endeavor of systematic CA-based intervention is the Conversation Analytic Role-play Method (CARM) developed by Elizabeth Stokoe (Stokoe, 2014). Based on conversation analysis of real-time interaction between a variety of organizations and their clients, CARM focuses on what is more or less effective in communicative encounters and provides evidence-based communication skills training. A key component of a CARM workshop entails using audio or video recordings along with their transcripts to raise awareness of and invite discussions on certain target moments during an interaction, where more or less effective choices may be made that can lead to more or less desirable outcomes. Participants are invited to 'join' the real-time interaction as the on-screen transcripts unfold along with their audio/video recordings. The transcript and recording are then stopped and 'frozen' at key 'choice points' to allow for participation and experimentation before what actually happened is revealed for further reflection.

CA for ELT (English Language Teaching)

By providing a fine-grained depiction of teacher conduct in the moment-by-moment unfolding of classroom reality and making evident the complexity and multimodality of such conduct, CA has also offered illuminating insights into the 'amazingly complex and demanding interactional and pedagogical work in the classroom' (Seedhouse, 2004, p. 265) or what Hall (2019) refers to as 'specialized work of L2 teaching' that requires 'a range of complex specialized repertoires composed of a wide array of multilingual, multimodal semiotic resources for taking action' (p. 228). At the same time, compared to the great strides made to bring CA findings to practitioners in various institutional contexts, the impact of CA in applied linguistics and in education more broadly has remained minimal—despite the growing body of robust classroom-based CA research (e.g., Kunitz, Sert, & Markee, forthcoming; Markee, 2000; Salaberry & Kunitz, 2019; Seedhouse, 2004; Sert, 2015; Walsh, 2006; Waring, 2016, 2019).

In describing how social epidemics work, Gladwell (2000) notes the need for Connectors, Mavens, and Salesmen to bring any innovation to its tipping point because they are the 'translators' who 'take ideas and information from a highly specialized world and translate them into a language the rest of us can understand' (p. 200). In applied linguistics and TESOL, there is at the moment no accumulative and collective resource, aside from a few monographs along with numerous book chapters and journal articles scattered across the field, from which one could obtain classroom conversation analytic research potentially applicable to teacher training. The Maven or the information specialist who voraciously gathers the growing body of relevant CA research and organizes it into digestible forms for teacher education is yet to arrive. Also absent from the scene is the Salesman who does the persuasion by demonstrating the usefulness of such research findings. Being the Maven and the Salesman for CA-based classroom research is a central aim of this book.

Evidence-based teacher training is not new in applied linguistics and TESOL. What the micro-analysis of CA research on classroom interaction brings into sharp relief, however, is the complex professional work teachers do (Hall, 2019) on a moment-to-moment basis—work that goes beyond what has been captured in traditional discussions of teaching skills, such as the macro tasks of lesson planning or activity design and the micro activities of informing, questioning, or assessing. In the second-by-second unfolding of classroom interaction, the language teacher allocates turns, builds rapport, maintains order, and promotes or curtails student participation while at the same time engaging a variety of verbal and visible means to teach pronunciation, explain vocabulary, elucidate tense and aspect, sort out tricky problems of understanding, and work with emerging learner initiatives and responses. Clearly, such highly contingent professional work requires the teacher to mobilize a complex interplay of multimodal resources in managing simultaneous demands such as engaging student attention while handling technical problems, attending to the individual without neglecting the group, and striking a delicate balance between maintaining the pedagogical focus and encouraging student participation. In this book, we propose, and illustrate how to implement, a framework for reflecting upon such micro-moments of classroom interaction as an integral component of language teacher education.

CONCEPTUALIZING THE MICRO: THE FAB FRAMEWORK

While CA clearly holds a goldmine of resources for revolutionizing language teacher education, there still remains the question of what exactly lies in those micro-moments of classroom interaction. If reflection is a key component of language teacher education, how can CA change the way we engage in reflection? What exact micro-moments do we want our teachers to reflect on to allow for micro-intervention? In this section, we offer a systematic conceptualization of these micro-moments through what we propose as the FAB framework: fostering an inviting environment, attending to learner voice, and balancing competing demands.

Our FAB framework is a practice-oriented re-conceptualization of Waring's (2016) three principles of pedagogical interaction:

(1) Competence: achieving competence entails assuming competence.
(2) Complexity: teacher talk is multivocalic (i.e., imbued with multiple voices).
(3) Contingency: teaching requires being responsive to the moment.

As over a decade of conversation analytic work in a variety of pedagogical contexts has shown, learners take every opportunity to assert, maintain, and defend their competence, and effective teaching involves knowing how to nurture that delicate concern by assuming competence. In addition, the complexity of teacher talk lies in the fact that every bit of teacher conduct can accomplish multiple actions, and such multivocality can be either an impediment to or a resource for promoting learning: sending conflicting messages impedes, but balancing competing demands facilitates. Finally, teaching requires the skill to be responsive as the teacher addresses the simultaneity of the moment, adjusts to the shifting demand of the moment, and preserves the integrity of the moment.

While the three C's constitute an empirically grounded theory of how pedagogical interactions work in real time, and as such, offer a guide to look or a way of seeing that can potentially transform behavior and inspire actionable undertakings, they do not directly engage such undertakings. 'Achieving competence entails assuming competence,' for example, does not articulate for the teacher or teacher educator what constitutes a practical goal in honing one's craft. Thus, although the conceptualization of FAB begins with the three principles of pedagogical interaction and integrates many elements of those principles, it is driven by a fundamentally different kind of concern. Rather than offer an understanding of pedagogical interaction, FAB targets behavior change in pedagogical interaction through micro-reflection. Therefore, with a solid grounding in the three theoretical principles of pedagogical interaction, the three components of FAB represent a reconceptualization of these three principles by way of specifying the goals of teacher development that would account for a broader spectrum of expertise intrinsic to the practical work of teaching, and in particular, to the management of interaction in this work:

(1) _f_oster an inviting environment;
(2) _a_ttend to learner voices;
(3) _b_alance competing demands.

A key aspect of managing interaction to optimize learning is to foster an environment that invites participation and exploration. This can be done by validating student contributions, maximizing student potentials, neutralizing asymmetries, encouraging exploratory talk, and finally, providing structure and clarity. After all, a confusing environment is not an inviting one. While **foster an inviting environment** focuses on the teacher's ability to maximize participation and exploration, **attend to learner voices** speaks to the skill of working with learner contributions in situ as they participate and explore, as opposed to delivering prepackaged information regardless of the specific needs of specific students at specific times, or what Karen Johnson refers to as 'Teach off your students, not at them' (Johnson & Dellagenlo, 2013, p. 432). As will be demonstrated, attending to student voices in real time requires the astuteness and agility to hear layered messages, offer tailored assistance, follow students' leads, and shape learner understandings starting with an accurate and true appreciation for learner logic. Finally, a more overarching challenge for managing interaction in the messy realities of actual classrooms involves the need to *balance* such *competing demands* as navigating attention between the individual and the group, ensuring depth of understanding within time constraints, promoting extended and yet even participation, implementing instruction while building rapport, and enforcing structure without discouraging play and experimentation. As daunting as this may sound, CA offers descriptions of concrete interactional moves through which such a balance may be achieved, such as assimilating learner voice, alluding to the institutional frame, engaging in ironic teasing, deploying gaze shifts, and the like.

Admittedly, with its focus on managing interaction, the FAB framework does not tell the story of everything about (language) teaching, and most likely, neither does it tell the story of everything about managing the interaction in (language) teaching. It is, however, built upon a substantial empirical foundation that absorbs a broad base of relevant conversation analytic research so far, and as such, offers an exciting, if not comprehensive, new way of cultivating reflective practices for language teachers and teacher educators. Finally, there is no doubt that the FAB classroom can look many different ways and take on many different shapes, and in this book, we do our best to portray those ways and shapes as we attempt, with our own conversation analytic lens, the monumental task of 'bearing witness to teaching and teachers' (Hansen, 2017, p. 7).

DOCUMENTING THE MICRO: THE TRANSCRIPTION SYSTEM

In order to document the micro-moments, we use a transcription system to visually represent what happens in real time. The idea is that when you write something down, you pay attention to it. We have also found that carefully reading a transcription helps us learn how to carefully pay attention to what is going on while we are teaching. Below, we look at some of the different kinds of information we can present in transcriptions. As we shall see, the transcription system captures not just what is said, but also how it is said in terms of qualities like volume, pitch, speed, and intonation as well as the timing of talk such as silence and simultaneous talk. It also captures physical actions, which are often just as important as the words we use. We begin with a bare-bone transcript that simply records what is said during a simple exchange in a lower-level adult ESL classroom, where the students are practicing answers to simple questions about people's lives. In the transcript, TC represents 'teacher,' and ST stands for a specific student's name. Feel free to use any name for the student as you read:

(1) live in new york [Waring classroom data—bare-bone]
01   TC: Okay, ST, where do they live?
02   ST: Uh they live New York.
03   TC: They one more time.
04   ST: They they live in New York.
05   TC: Okay, they live in New York, right?
06   ST: Yes.

The transcript looks very clean and readable. The problem is that it does not faithfully represent what actually happens in the moment. For one thing, talk is delivered in particular 'tones'—loud or quiet, high or low, and in particular intonation contours—rising (as when we ask a yes/no question), falling (as when we give factual information or orders), or continuing (as when we finish an adverbial clause such as *If I do this now*). We use punctuations in our transcription system to indicate intonation: period for falling, question mark for rising, and comma for continuing. Besides the intonation contour for an entire unit, particular words may be said in louder or quieter volumes: we use capital letters to indicate loudness, and degree signs for quiet volume. Particular words may also be said in raised or lowered pitches: we use an upward arrow to indicate raised pitch, and downward arrow lowered pitch. Any underlined portion of a word just means that word is delivered with some general sense of emphasis or stress. Sometimes a word might be cut-off before it is fully articulated, and that delivery feature is presented by a dash as in *well-*. Because capital letters are used to indicate loud volume in CA transcription, we don't capitalize the first letter of any sentence or unit but do keep capitalization for proper nouns to avoid confusion.

Table 1.1 CA transcription—capturing tones and intonations

symbol	meaning
.	(period) falling intonation
?	(question mark) rising intonation
,	(comma) continuing intonation
-	(dash) abrupt cut-off
<u>w</u>ord	(underlining) stress
<u>wo</u>rd	the more underlining the greater the stress
WORD	(all caps) loud speech
°word°	(degree signs) quiet speech
↑word	(upward arrow) raised pitch
↓word	(downward arrow) lowered pitch

Task 1

Using the transcription notations in Table 1.1, read Extract (2) below with all its delivery markings. Note that reading punctuations as intonation marks might take some time to get used to. Work with a partner if possible. Think about what extra information these delivery details can offer us in terms of teaching and learning.

(2) live in new york [Waring classroom data—tone and intonation]

01	TC:	okay, ST, where do they live.
02	ST:	uh they °live° New York.
03	TC:	they one more time.
04	ST:	they- they live IN New York.
05	TC:	okay, they live in New Y↑ork.right?
06	ST:	yes.

We might note that the quiet delivery of *live* in line 02 might indicate that the student is approaching something he is not entire sure of, and the loud delivery of *in* in line 04 is his way of highlighting for the teacher what he is doing differently now from what he did earlier—his self-correction.

Timing is another aspect of delivery that CA transcriptions capture. First of all, there is the issue of how fast or slow something is said. We use colons to indicate the elongations of sounds; if an entire unit is said in slower pace, we include that entire unit in < >; we flip the directions of the arrows to indicate faster speech > <. There is also the issue of timing in terms of what one says in relation to what someone else has just said or is saying. Do we start talking before the other has finished, immediately upon the other's completion, or one second after the other is done? We use numbers (or a period) in parentheses to indicate the length of silence, equal sign to indicate beginning any next unit without any break, and lined-up square brackets to indicate the beginning and ending of simultaneous talk (and/or conduct).

Table 1.2 CA transcription—capturing timing

symbol	meaning
::	(colon(s)) prolonging of sound
>word<	(more than and less than) quicker speech
<word>	(less than and more than) slower speech
[ ]	(lined up brackets) beginning and ending of simultaneous/overlapping speech and or conduct
=	(equal sign) beginning of any next unit without a break
(2.4)	(number in parentheses) length of silence in 10th of a second
(.)	(period in parenthesis) micro-pause of 0.2 second or less

Task 2

Using the transcription notations in Tables 1.1 and 1.2, read Extract (3) below with all its additional delivery markings. Work with a partner if possible. Think about what extra information these additional markings tell us about teaching and learning.

(3) live in new york [Waring classroom data—timing]
```
01    TC:      >okay, < ST, where do they live.
02             (0.8)
03    ST:      u::h the:y °live° >New York.<
04    TC:      the::y >one more time.<
05    ST:      they- the:y li:ve (0.2) IN New York.
06    TC:      >okay, they live in New Y↑ork.<[=right?]
07    ST:                                     [  yes.  ]
```

We might observe, for example, that the student's response is not immediately forthcoming, as marked by the (0.8) second silence in line 02 as well as the elongations of *uh* and *they* in line 03.

In addition to all the delivery details of verbal conduct, more and more conversation analysts are realizing that our non-verbal conduct is also extremely important in how we understand each other and make ourselves understood. Including descriptions of such non-verbal conduct is now a standard practice in CA transcriptions. We use italicized words to indicate the non-verbal. More specifically, if the non-verbal follows the speaker's talk, the description is placed after that talk; if it accompanies the speaker's talk, it is placed on an unnumbered line below that talk with square brackets to indicate simultaneity; if it is in response to another's talk, it is placed on a numbered line (with square brackets if applicable).

Table 1.3 CA transcription—capturing the non-verbal

symbol	meaning
(comment)	transcriptionist comment
word on numbered line	(italics) visual conduct <u>not</u> co-occurring with own talk (or silence)
word on unnumbered line	(italics) visual conduct co-occurring with own talk (or silence)

Task 3

Using the transcription notations in Tables 1.1–1.3, read Extract (4) below with all its added non-verbal markings. Work with a partner if possible. Think about what these non-verbal details may add to our understanding of teaching and learning in that moment.

(4) live in new york [Waring classroom data—non-verbal]

```
01   TC:     >okay, < ST, [where do they live.
02   ST:               [looks up to TC
03           (0.8)
04   ST:     u::h the:y °live° >New York.<
05   TC:     the::y >one more time.<hand behind ear
06   ST:     [they- the:y li:ve (0.2) [IN New York.
             [gaze away            [gaze up to TC
07   TC:     >okay, they live in New Y↑ork.<[=right?]
08   ST:                               [ yes.  ]
```

As we can see, in line 02, the student looks up immediately upon hearing his name. In other words, the (0.8) silence in line 03 is clearly not a sign of not paying attention. In line 06, he also gazes away first as he struggles to formulate his correction and brings his gaze back to the teacher at the same time as he produces the correction—the inserted *in*. We also see the teacher's hand-behind-ear gesture after saying *one more time* in line 05. It is interesting to note how this gesture in combination with the request to repeat is treated by the student as an invitation to self-correct.

The full transcription system can be found in Appendix A, but with the brief exercises above, we hope to have at least whetted your appetite for finding and appreciating the details of micro-moments—with this basic set of symbols that you will be seeing again and again. Throughout the book, we will also provide reminders, as we introduce each extract, of what some of the less intuitive symbols represent. By the time you finish this book, you should be able to produce your own CA transcripts for micro-reflection!

Task 4

Returning to Extract (4) above, try to find four different symbols and explain what they mean.
(1)
(2)
(3)
(4)

PLAN OF THE BOOK

In the next three chapters (2–4), we take you on a hands-on, guided tour of FAB, with a specific focus on how each component serves as a basis for developing our abilities to engage in micro-reflection. As noted earlier, in each chapter, we not only invite you to notice the specific practices for achieving a goal such as fostering an inviting environment, we also provide an assortment of structured activities, to complete the cycle of micro-reflection, for you to try out your own abilities to observe and experiment. We draw upon a wider range of exemplars from pedagogical contexts beyond the language classroom, based on our firm belief that there are elements of 'good teaching' that are recognizable and worth duplicating across age groups and disciplinary boundaries.

Chapter 5 begins with an exhibit that demonstrates how the three aspects of the FAB framework come together in the 'messy' reality of the classroom. Indeed, in real life, the three aspects of FAB often converge and are managed in a single moment or within a single interaction. Thus, it is via micro-reflection that teachers can move from these ideals of FAB to an integrated practice that constitutes the exciting complexity of teaching.

The concluding chapter situates the discussion of micro-reflection within the larger context of language teacher education. In particular, we discuss the implications of micro-reflection for teacher assessment, its affordances for teacher empowerment, and its leverage to illuminate and magnify the humanity of the classroom. The chapter ends with an argument for moving from micro-reflection towards a 'micro-revolution' of classroom interaction, suggesting that changing teacher-student dynamics and promoting student agency begins, ultimately, at the micro-level.

You will notice some repetitive formats and wordings throughout Chapters 2–5 as these chapters are designed to be used independently without following any particular order. If your interest is in balancing competing demands, for example, feel free to skip Chapter 2 and go directly to Chapter 4. You can also go directly from Chapter 1 to Chapter 5 to get a quick sense of how the various practices work together before delving into the specifics of each FAB element. Finally, we would also emphasize the importance of working slowly through each chapter and completing all the exercises—repeatedly if necessary. After all, it is in the actual doing of micro-reflection that we become micro-reflectors.

Chapter 2
Foster an Inviting Environment

In this chapter, we use the cycle of micro-reflection to discuss the first step of the FAB framework: <u>F</u>ostering an inviting environment. It may seem obvious that classrooms should feel inviting. Unfortunately, all too many students (and teachers as well) seem to spend their days in an intimidating atmosphere that silences rather than invites. For us, an inviting environment is one where students feel safe enough to fully engage in classroom activities. The issue of student participation and engagement is particularly important for those of us working with second language learners, since considerable research suggests that student output and negotiation of meaning are crucial for language learning (Long, 1983; Swain, 1985; for a useful overview, see Gass & Mackay, 2006). We start here then, because an inviting classroom is one where student learning is more likely to occur. And as we hope you'll see, fostering this kind of environment may require rethinking some of our assumptions about what teachers are 'supposed' to do. In our experience, teachers teach the way that they were taught. This is one reason that the cycle of micro-reflection can be helpful, in that it asks us to notice our patterns and then make conscious choices about whether we want to continue them. Below, we discuss three ways in which teachers can **foster an inviting environment**: (1) being clear; (2) being open; and (3) being equal. For each of these, we move through the cycle of micro-reflection described in Chapter 1. We start with noticing what kinds of teacher-actions do (and do not) lead to the kind of classroom atmosphere we are aiming for. Next, we move on to changing, offering suggestions for how to use micro-reflection as we work on fostering an inviting environment in our classrooms.

BEING CLEAR

An inviting environment is an environment where students are clear about what they are supposed to do and why they are doing it. Most of us can remember the uncomfortable feeling of not knowing exactly what a teacher was asking for. It is this kind of anxiety that we can avoid by being clear. To put it differently, we can help students feel free to participate by making sure that they understand both the material we are covering, and what is expected of them in the classroom environment.

Noticing

Not being clear

One way to understand being clear is to think about what it means to not be clear. The example below shows some of the ways teachers can engender confusion for their students, thus creating an *un*inviting environment. This excerpt is taken from a tutoring session where the tutor (TR) is attempting to help a 2nd-grade tutee (TT) learn about words that end in 'ee,' such as 'tree,' 'bee,' and—the centerpiece of the following excerpt—'manatee.' Together, the two have spelled the first part of the word 'manatee' (M-A-N-A-T-). Now, the teacher is hoping that her student will come up with the last two letters, which are the focus of this lesson. As the excerpt begins, tutor and tutee are sitting around a table. On the table is a book (called *The tree, the bee, and me*), a white board, and a few plastic toys, including a tree. (Transcription note: $ = smiley voice.)

(1) what did they end in [Waring & Hruska, 2012, p. 292]

```
01   TR:    [mana:,
            [picks up board and tilts to TT's direction
02          [tee::?        ]
            [glances at TT's board and withdraws own
03   TT:    [$mh↑hmm] [nnnnn$]
04   TR:                [okay,    ] wha[t did- ]
05   TT:                                  [(yeh.)]
06   TR:    what did all [these
                          [reaches for tree
07          [picks up and repositions tree
08   TT:    [tre[e:::::::: ]
09   TR:        [letter-] what did they
10          [end in.
            [brings closer green book with 'tree' and 'bee' and 'me'
11   TT:    [tree:
            [looks to green book
```

In line 01, the teacher starts by repeating the word *manatee*, first pausing before the end of the word, and then drawing out the final syllable, ending with the upturn of a question (Koshik, 2002). This may be an attempt, in and of itself, to get the tutee to finish spelling the word. The tutee, however, replies with a smiley *mhhmm* (line 03)—not the hoped-for letters 'E' 'E.' The teacher then starts to ask a question in line 04, saying *what did*. We then see the teacher rework her question two more times, as she first asks *what did all these* and then *what did they end in* (lines 06, 09, & 10). She also says the word *letter* in line 09.

The first thing we notice is how these questions are constructed. It's not really clear what the teacher is referring to when she says the words *these* (line 06) and *they* (line 09). For instance, she could be talking about the words on the cover of the book, which include *tree* and *bee,* but also *me*. In addition, the phrase *end in* is also unclear, particularly for a young student who is new to the idea of spelling. The teacher could be talking about the sound the words end in, rather than the letters. And, even if the student figures out that she is supposed to spell, it's not clear that she should provide two letters, rather than one. Essentially, then, we see a problem with unclear references here. As Waring & Hruska (2012) note, teachers working with second language learners are often told to avoid pronouns, and to use proper nouns instead. We see why that might a good idea in this extract!

When learners do not understand a teacher's words, they often look to her gestures for clues. However, in this case, that strategy seems to lead to more confusion. As the tutor tries to finish her question, she reaches first for the toy tree, and then for the book (lines 06 & 07, 10). Her tutee carefully monitors these actions. We can see this attentiveness in her 'answer' in line 08, when she narrates the teacher's action of playing with an object by naming the object—*tree*, and then by her gaze shift in line 11, when she shifts her eyes towards the book the teacher is touching. In other words, the tutee does not understand the connections that the tutor is making between these objects and the questions. For her, the tutor's gestures simply suggest that she should name the object. We do not show the end of the interaction, but, in fact, it takes almost the whole session for the tutor to explain her spelling goal.

One overarching point here is that most students want to understand their teacher. This means that they are listening and observing very closely, and when we add extraneous information, in the form of a cluttered environment, unclear words, or meaningless gestures, we make their work as students much more difficult.

One area where clarity is often lacking is in giving instructions. For instance, Seedhouse (2008) describes the 'mismatch' (p. 43) between what teachers want students to do and what actually occurs, arguing that one reason for such difficulties is a lack of clarity regarding the overall point of a lesson. Johnson (1995) makes a similar point, writing that 'second language students can become confused about what is expected of them, or how they should participate' (p. 163). Thus, one way to be clear is to make sure that students understand the big picture—that they have a sense of how each step in an activity, or each phrase or gesture used by a teacher, relates to a larger goal. At the same time, we saw above how important it is to also attend to individual words, phrases, and gestures. In other words, being clear involves both the big picture and the fine details of our actions. Below, we offer examples of two strategies teachers might use to handle the fine art of being clear.

> **Strategies for being clear:** (1) frame and focus; (2) break it down.

Frame and focus

We start by discussing two related practices: framing and providing a focus. Both are related to giving students a clear sense of where to put their attention during a given activity. First, a teacher can **frame** an activity as it begins, helping students understand both their purpose, and the primary action they are about to engage in. As we will see, framing is somewhat different from explaining an objective, a process with which most teachers are familiar. Rather than telling students what they will learn, a frame tells them what they will *do*, and is usually formed using an action verb. Secondly, throughout each activity, the teacher can provide constant and regular reminders of **focus**, using a combination of gesture, paralinguistic cues, and talk that shows students where, in a complex setting, to place their attention.

To better understand these strategies, let's look at an example. We start in a bilingual (French-English) kindergarten, where five children are sitting around a table with their teacher (TC). On the table is a plastic tray, a jug of lavender-tinted water, and an empty water-bottle with a spout at the bottom. The students (ST1, ST2, etc.) have spent the past few days doing experiments with water, and this particular experiment is designed to see if the group can make water move upwards in a container. Most of the original interaction took place in French, but the conversation has been translated into English for ease of reading. Take a look at the lines in bold type and see if you can catch how this teacher frames her upcoming activity.

(2a) water [Creider, 2016, p. 81]
01   TC: **we're going to see [when the water starts**
                        [*finger point towards E*

02		to jump. and [at what level we see the water.
		[*touches side of jug*
03		*pours water into jug.*
04	ST1:	n[ow!
05	ST2:	[smiles, *points at jug*
06	TC:	whoa!
07	ST2:	*leans in, points to jug*
08	ST?:	ah tsssssss
09	ST1:	*leans in towards center of table*

In line 01, the teacher starts off by explaining what the class is going to do, namely *see*. In other words, she makes clear that the action she expects of students: to look at something. She then goes on to specify, very carefully, what they are looking for: *when the water starts to jump* (lines 01 & 02). Notice the use of the word *when* in this sentence. The teacher could have said something like 'We're going to notice the water jump.' However, the point of this exercise is to figure out at what point the weight of water being poured into a container causes the water already in the container to move upwards. In other words, the important scientific question is *when* the water starts to jump, not simply the fact that it does so.

We also notice that the teacher waits to begin pouring water until she has completed her framing statement. This seemingly minor detail ensures that students can focus on her talk, rather than getting distracted by the water. In these brief lines, then, TC gives students a clear picture of what this activity entails, what her expectations are, and how her students can meet those expectations. And, in line 04, we see ST1 respond appropriately, as he shouts *now!* when the water starts to move. Other students (and the teacher) show their excitement about the water in the lines that follow.

Now that this teacher has given her students a frame, let's notice how she provides a focus, or clues about what's important in this busy environment. Notice the timing of words and gestures throughout this extract.

(2b) water [Creider, 2016, p. 81]

10	TC:	it's stronger than yesterday in fact.
11		*puts jug down*
12		**[look now the level is high and now the**
		[*points to jug*
13		**level is low.**
14	ST?:	that was coowel!
15	ST3:	*points towards jug*

16	TC:	do you want to see again
17	ST4:	*leans in towards center of table*
18	TC:	**are you ready?**
19	ST?:	yes.
20	TC:	**[look. the level here. and**
		[*points to jug, plastic cup in other hand*
21		**[how it jumps.**
		[*moves hand up jug*

Do you see how the teacher times her words and gestures throughout this interaction? In line 12, exactly as she says the word *look*, the teacher shows her students where to look, as she points at the jug. (Notice that before she said *look*, the teacher put the jug down, as if in preparation for pointing.) Then, in line 18, the teacher prepares her students for what will come next, by asking if they're ready. If a pointing gesture tells students where to focus their eyes in the physical environment, asking if everyone is ready is like a temporal 'point'—it helps students know *when* to pay attention. The word *look* serves a similar purpose throughout this extract. The teacher could simply have described what she was seeing: 'now the level is high and now the level is low.' Instead, by prefacing her observation with the word *look* (line 12), she helps her students to focus before she points out what she sees. And, she accomplishes this with great economy, by simply adding one word to her turns. Finally, in line 21, as she says *how it jumps*, the teacher moves her hand up the jug, mimicking the jumping action.

Our final section of this transcript offers another example of the 'warning' we saw above. Once again, we're going to focus on the section in bold type below.

(2c) water [Creider, 2016, p. 81]

22	TC:	[*starts to pour water into jug*
23	SS:	[*gaze on jug*
24	ST5:	the water's pushing.
25	TC:	*finishes pouring*
26		**so. look now.** *puts cup down.*
27		**[the water is <u>h</u>igh.**
		[*points to jug*
28	ST2:	[*leans in*
29	ST1:	[oh look!
		[*points towards water*
30	ST5:	it's really gonna be (( )/spot)!
31	ST4:	*leans in towards center of table*
32	TC:	wow.

This section includes yet another example of words and gesture working together (line 27). But we also want to notice line 26. Here, our teacher once again warns her students that it's time to pay attention—this time by explicitly telling them to look *now*. We include these additional examples to emphasize the idea that the same skillful practices can be repeated as many times as is needed, even within a very small expanse of time.

To sum up, providing a **frame** and a **focus** means using words and gestures to show students exactly what aspects of their environment are important. And there are many ways to accomplish these strategies, not all of which have been shown here. For instance, we have observed teachers using elongation, tone, and pauses to emphasize the important words in a sentence, thus helping students focus on key concepts or key language. Teachers also might use facial expressions and eye gaze, both to provide the kinds of warnings we discuss above, and to emphasize either words or places in the classroom environment.

Break it down

The next strategy in this section is **breaking it down.** This skill has to do with how teachers can split a complex activity or idea into small, manageable chunks. In the extract that follows, we see a teacher do just this, as she helps her adult, intermediate-level ESL students better understand the meaning of a word. As the extract begins, the teacher (TC) is seated, with approximately 10 students (ST1, ST2, etc.) at desks in two concentric horseshoes around their teacher. The class has just finished going over a vocabulary worksheet in pairs, and the extract begins as their teacher points out a particular word on their papers. Although this conversation actually only lasts for about two and half minutes, it's a quite long transcript, so we are going to look at it in several pieces. (In other words, we are following our own advice, and **breaking it down!**) Our focus is on the bold lines in each section:

(3a) upset [Boblett, 2020]

```
01   TC:        [do you see the word?
                [looks down at paper
02   ST1:       upset?
03   TC:        upset. do you know [what the word is?]
04   ST2, ST3:                     [    nodding    ]
05   TC:        upset.
06   ST2:       I use [the word.]
07   SS:              [   ()   ]
                      [ nodding ]
```

As the extract begins TC asks if students are familiar with the word *upset* (lines 01–03). We notice that her question is formed in an interesting way. Rather than asking if students know what the word means, she asks if they know what it *is*. Most language teachers can attest to the fact that it takes real skill—and language ability—to explain the meaning of a word in another language (or even in our own language!). However, there seem to be a variety of possible responses to the question of what a word *is*—for instance, what part of speech is the word? How do we use it? When do we use it? And, in line 06, we see that ST2 responds, not by telling us about the word, but by simply announcing that she uses *the word*. Thus, we have spent quite a bit of time simply establishing this word as something worth discussing. (You might notice how this relates to our discussion of **framing** and **focusing**.) Let's see what the teacher does next.

(3b) upset [Boblett, 2020]

08	**TC:**	[**oh** you **u:se** this. oh **good**
		[*to ST2, surprised look*
09		[then you can tell us about it.] give us ah:
10	ST2:	[hhh. (*breathy laughs*)]
11	**TC:**	**give us maybe a- tell us a little**
12		**story or a- paint us a picture. when you (0.4) when you (.)**
13		**give us an example of a time**
14		***checks paper* you feel upset.**
(lines deleted)		
29	ST2	because before I use shocked (.) but I prefer upset.

The teacher responds with energy (Did you notice the emphasis on *oh* and *good*, and the elongated vowel in *use* in line 08?) and then quickly asks the student for more information. However, she doesn't ask for a definition. Instead, she tells the student to *tell us a little story, paint us a picture, give us an example* (lines 11–14). TC seems to be focusing on giving her students a sense of when we might use this word. After ST2 explains that *upset* is a word she always remembers (not shown), the student offers a related word: *shocked*. In the next small section, the teacher starts to ask for a definition, but stops and does something else instead. Let's see what that is.

(3c) upset [Boblett, 2020]

30	**TC:**	**upset. *looks around* anyone kno- can you (.) let's try to**
31		**put together a**
32		(0.2)

33	ST4:	I- I uh al[ways]
34	**TC:**	[**a def-**] **°mm°** ***turns to ST4***
35	ST4:	tell my daughter that I am really upset with her
36		because she never clean her bedroom.
37	TC:	*nods*
38	SS:	[*laughing*]
39	TC:	*gaze around group* [it's upse-]
40	ST4:	I [can't ( )] mess.
41	TC:	[usually] [yeah.]
42	ST6:	[*laughing*]
43	TC:	*to ST4* I remember those days. my daughter *points up diagonal*
44		is now *pushes up* -a million [miles] away, she's in she's in France
45	ST4:	[upset]
46	TC:	but I <u>do</u> re[member those] upset. *turns to group* it's
47	ST4:	[heh heh heh]
48	S?:	°hehe°
49	**TC:**	**it's it's kind of *big circle to hand clasp* a mixture of**
50		***looks around at group* a lot of different [emotions right?**
51	SS:	[*murmurs, low talk*

TC finally seems ready to suggest that it's time for a definition (see her start to say *def-* in line 34), but she does it in such a way that makes room for plenty of careful work. Rather than simply offering a definition, or asking how to define the word, she uses the phrase *put together* (line 31), which seems to suggest that a definition needs to be put together, step-by-step. However, before TC can finish, ST4 comes up with a time when she uses *upset*—when she has to tell her daughter to clean her bedroom. After sympathizing with her student, TC finally, in lines 49 and 50, starts to define the word. First, she explains that it's a mixture of different emotions. What happens next is our favorite part of this extract. Take a look at the bold lines below, and see what kind of pattern you notice.

(3d) upset [Boblett, 2020]

52	ST6:	angry.
53	ST5:	ah::
54	TC:	and maybe anger?
55	ST6:	angry.
56	TC:	so what else? [you're angry?
		[*to ST6*

57	SS:	[*various responses*
58	ST2:	[surprised?
59	**TC:**	*turns to ST2* **maybe maybe surprised?**
60	ST1:	sad?
61	**TC:**	*turns to ST1* **maybe sad?**
62	ST4:	*hand up* -tired?
63	**TC:**	[**maybe tired?**
		[*turns to and gestures to ST4*
64	ST5:	*nodding*
65	**TC:**	**if you mix all these things so it's** *to ST4* **-a little angry,**
66		**a little tired a little (.) a little**
67		**[(0.2)**
		[*looks around group*
68		**uh: [surprised? all those things together? (.) you get upset.**
		[*to ST3*
69		**it's really a good kind of** *both hands make circles* **-all purpose**
70		*smiling, looks around* **-<u>neg</u>ative [uh:: (h)adject(h)ive.**
71	SS:	[*scattered laughter*

Perhaps the first thing we can notice here is how collaborative this section is. Together, teacher and students create a list of the different emotions that can make up *upset*. Each time a student names an emotion, the teacher repeats their suggestion, adding the adverb *maybe* (lines 59, 61, & 63). Interestingly, this pattern seems to suggest that not just the word, but the feeling itself can be **broken down** into several, smaller components. Finally, in lines 65 through 68, the teacher reiterates that the word includes a *mix* of *angry, tired,* and *surprised*. Often, this kind of repetition can be a part of **breaking it down**, as we take the time to go over important material more than once. Finally, after this careful description of component parts, TC offers more information to her students, including both the part-of-speech and the emotional valence of the word (lines 69 & 70).

To sum up, then, this discussion of a single word starts by setting the stage, and making sure that everyone is clear about what the word is. (We also notice that the careful repetition at the beginning of this extract would be helpful for any students with questions about pronunciation.) Then we hear similar words, times when the word is used, the various 'parts' of the word, and finally part of speech and emotional valence. Thus, **breaking it down** involves moving step-by-step through the component parts of an idea—or in this case, a word. Along with being an important strategy when talking about complex ideas or vocabulary, we have also seen teachers **break it down** when they give instructions, carefully describing each step of an activity before moving on to the next. Being clear, then, seems to involve not making assumptions about student understanding, and making sure that we are explicit, both about expectations, and about new ideas. A first step may involve reflecting on planned activities before class. We can then be ready to frame the activity using action verbs, and also know what words (or places) we want to help students focus on. Some teachers like to think about examples or illustrations they could use ahead of time. That said, we find that much of the work of being clear requires careful attention to our moment-by-moment choices. For instance, we can remember to provide warnings that gather student attention and to use gestures carefully. In general, it's all too easy to accidentally practice not being clear— for instance, by gesturing to one object while talking about another! Below, we list some specific resources teachers can use in the service of being clear.

Resources for Being Clear

(1) announce upcoming activities with action verbs (e.g., *we're gonna look*)
(2) set apart focal words with pauses, lengthened vowels, and tone
(3) provide warnings to gather student attention (e.g., *look*, or *are you ready?*)
(4) gesture (point) towards important places in the environment
(5) time gestures to match words
(6) give or ask for examples and illustrations
(7) repeat key words or ideas
(8) use phrases such as 'put together' to invite multiple perspectives
(9) use words such as 'maybe' to avoid suggesting a single final answer

Changing

So far, we have focused on noticing what types of teacher conduct are conducive to being clear, and what interactional resources (verbal and visible) can be recruited to assemble such conduct. To move from noticing to changing, we now offer a series of guided exercises to facilitate this transition.

What to look for

1. Based on your experiences as a student, a teacher, or an observer, what would you say might be three signs of a teacher being clear? More specifically, what would be some of the features of student conduct (e.g., starting to work without a problem)? What would be some of the features of the teacher's conduct? You can write your notes in the box below:

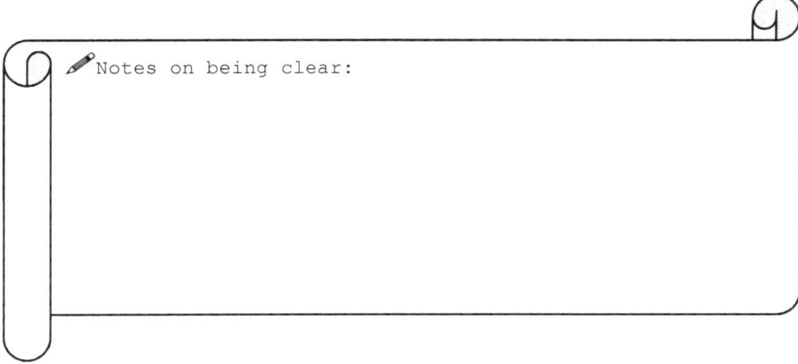

2. Consider the following extract, where a tutor (TR) is explaining a math game to a four-year-old tutee (TT). The focus of the game is the number four. Players take turns laying down between 1 and 4 chips, and their partner then has to lay down however many additional chips will add up to exactly four. What are some of the observable signs of being clear or not being clear?

    (4) we wanna make four [Creider, 2012, p. 56]
    01 TR: [ok. here's the game
                [*taking four yellow chips in her hand*
    02   (0.8) [take them in your=
    03 TT: [*TT takes four red chips*
    04 TR: =hand
    05 TR: we wanna make [four
                            [*traces horizontal line with fingertip*
    06   together here.

What to think about

1. In our noticing section above, we have drawn attention to some strategies of not being clear, such as using gestures that conflict with talk, and of being clear, such as providing a frame. The lists are most definitely not exhaustive. Take a moment to focus on the idea of being clear and think of any other strategies (positive or negative) based on your experiences and/or observations as a teacher or a student. Be as specific as possible in your description of the strategy:

(a) When is it done (e.g., initiating or responsive position), how is it done, and what response(s) does it receive?
(b) What words, gestures, intonation, and timing are used in its delivery?
(c) What alternatives are available at the time of its production?

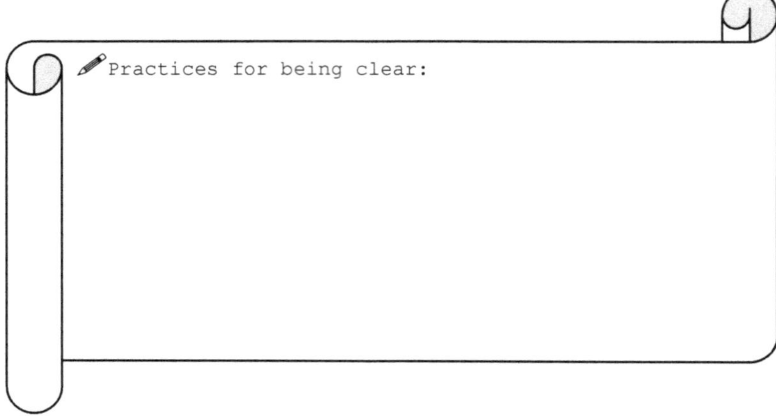

2. Consider the following extract, which is a small group activity in the same bilingual kindergarten we've already looked at in this chapter. Here, teacher and students are talking about different ways to make the number eight (2+6, 4+4, etc.). For each turn set in bold type, describe:
(a) what alternatives there might be;
(b) what the teacher does precisely (e.g., X as opposed to Y);
(c) what specific resources are used;
(d) in what way the teacher's conduct might be an example of being clear;
(e) how it is responded to;
(f) what other choices there might be at this juncture that would also be clear.

(5) eight [Creider, 2016, p. 82]
01 TC: today you're going to guess
(Lines omitted. TC asks a student not to touch chips.)
02   so today we're going to
03   make the combina[tions (0.6) of (.)
                                    [*eyes towards S1*
04   [eight
              [*raises eyebrow, eyes to S2*
05   how we can make the number eight

What to do

1. Based on the skills you have developed so far, observe an actual lesson (with a video-camera if possible) with a specific focus on strategies for (not) being clear. Organize your notes using the following table.

Strategies for being clear	
Strategies	Details
1. 2. 3.	(a) What could have been done differently at this particular moment in the interaction? (b) What is not being done, and why? (c) What exactly is being done, and how? (d) How is what is being done taken up by the participants in the data?
Strategies for not being clear	
Strategies	Details
1. 2. 3.	(a) What could have been done differently at this particular moment in the interaction? (b) What is not being done, and why? (c) What exactly is being done, and how? (d) How is what is being done taken up by the participants in the data?

2. Repeat the same exercise above with a video-recording of your own teaching and invite a colleague to either join the exercise or offer feedback on your own analysis.
3. With the observational materials you have now gathered (video recordings preferably), identify moments where the teacher does being clear, and try to work backwards to figure out what has been done to lead to that moment.
4. Try out specific strategies for being clear in your own class, one at a time. Make note of its effect in terms of specific student conduct. Make adjustments accordingly as you repeat the exercise.

BEING OPEN

Fostering an inviting environment also entails building a sense of openness within a structured pedagogical environment. This means creating a space where interaction is not driven by definitive and correct answers, and where uncertainties and experimentations are legitimized rather than censured. To follow our cycle of micro-reflection, as in the prior section, we move from noticing to changing.

With noticing, we invite you to think about how to create an environment that is open, drawing attention to the various strategies that may inhibit or promote that openness. Such noticing would set the stage for making subsequent changes in one's strategies. Changing, as noted above, entails a set of exercises that guide us through what to look for, what to think about, and what to do in others' and our own classes.

Noticing

Not being open

We first invite you to notice what not being open may look like in the classroom. More specifically, by way of illustration, we will walk you through three different scenarios. One scenario of not being open involves maintaining a singular focus on the teacher's own agenda without accommodating any unsolicited student contributions. In the midst of a student report on Thomas Edison the inventor, for example, a student might be sharing more than what the teacher has asked. The teacher then can find a way to assimilate this 'extra information' into the pedagogical activity (see Chapter 4 on Balancing) or to cut it short for the purpose of keeping intact her plan, as in the extract below. (Transcription notes: colon = elongation; dash = cut-off or abrupt stop; > < = quickened pace; underline = stress; question mark = rising intonation; period = falling intonation.)

(6) make the story short [Waring data]
```
01    ST:      (lines omitted) he moved to Michigan, and e::h he got a job as a::::
02             tele- telegra::
03    TC:      >oh yeah great thank you but I wanna jus'<
04             make the story short?
05    ST:      ah okay.
```

As can be seen, instead of letting the student continue with the extra information, the teacher rushes to close up the telling and explicitly announce her intention to make the story short (lines 03 & 04)—a decision that the student immediately accepts (line 05).

Not being open may also be observed in some of the most routine teacher talk that seems entirely innocuous. As teachers, for example, we select students to complete exercises, and we evaluate their answers, following the IRF (initiation-response-feedback) structure (Sinclair & Coulthard, 1975), as in the following familiar case. The students are completing an exercise of making sentences using the present progressive tense after reading a 'prompt' in the textbook. (Transcription notes: number in parentheses = length of silence in seconds; (.) = a micro pause less than 0.2 second.)

(7) excellent [Waring data; simplified]
01	TC:	*reads instructions for the next exercise*
02		number one. ST.
03	ST:	[oh really? I didn't know you were trying for the Olympics.
		[*reads*
04		how long (.) have you been trying (.) for the Olympics?
05	**TC:**	**good. how long have you been training for the Olympics.**
06		excellent.
07		(0.2)
08		number two.

Note that the teacher positively evaluates the student's answer (lines 05 & 06) and moves on to the next item (line 08). This neat and orderly initiation-response-feedback progression could constitute a 'dis-invitation' for sharing other possible answers and displaying potential confusion (Waring, 2008). As you may notice, no student talks during the (0.2) second gap in line 07. In one case documented in Waring (2009), a series of items that ran off smoothly turns out to be problematic for many, and this only becomes evident when one student launches a move, in close coordination with the teacher, out of the IRF sequences. The positive feedback, in other words, plays a role in closing, rather than opening up, a space for learning.

Finally, checking understanding may also be a way of inadvertently closing down any participation. In the following example, the teacher has just finished giving instructions for an upcoming dictation activity, and he checks understanding with *Do you have any questions?* in line 02.

(8) no questions [Waring data]
01		[(0.5)
		[*T approaches ST1 and ST2*
02	**TC:**	**[do you have any questions?**
		[*to ST1*
03	ST1:	no.
04	TC:	[very clear?
		[*to ST2*
05	ST2:	yes.

As it turns out, these understanding-checks are routinely treated by students as signaling the end of an activity (Waring, 2012), and as such, close rather than open up a space for any further negotiations. As we can see in the above extract, no student raises any questions or offers comments, and both ST1 and ST2 respond in ways that facilitate the closing of the sequence.

One theme lurking in these closing strategies appears to be the priority of moving through the lesson as planned and moving on. This is evident as well in Fagan's (2012) documentation of a novice teacher's practice of dealing with unexpected learner contributions, which get glossed over (e.g., with a quick *okay*) or quickly responded to as the teacher jumps in with a 'final answer' rather than work with the trouble as it emerges. This focus on the final or correct answer can create a closed environment where student talk is simply evaluated as right or wrong rather than welcomed and appreciated.

So far, we have considered a few examples of what not being open may look like in the classroom. As you may have noticed, these tend to be the most natural, seen-but-unnoticed teacher practices (e.g., asking questions and assessing responses). In particular, positive assessments and understanding-checks, ironically, both appear to be encouraging and welcoming at first glance. As such, doing the opposite, or being open, would involve breaking the mold of what we naturally and typically do and believe. For some novice teachers in particular, it would involve making a deliberate effort to engage in specific interactional work. We describe three strategies below.

> **Strategies for being open:** (1) engage in exploratory talk; (2) welcome student initiations; (3) appreciate student mistakes.

Engage in exploratory talk

Engaging in **exploratory talk** (Barnes, 1976/1992; Boblett, 2018; also see 'model exploration' in Fagan, 2013) is one way of being open. 'Exploratory talk,' a term coined by Barnes (1976/1992), exhibits a range of features that indicate work- or thinking-in progress, such as 'hesitations, back-pedaling, false starts, and disfluency' (Boblett, 2018, p. 261). In the segment below, we observe how modelling this kind of talk serves to open up a space for student participation. The class is in the midst of figuring out what words to stress in a sentence, and the particular sentence in question is 'He wants to help her forget.' Although it is not the pedagogical focus at the moment, the teacher notices something out of the ordinary with the verb help. Typically, we use the infinitive *to* to connect two verbs in a sentence, e.g., 'He tries <u>to</u> call her.' With the verb 'help,' however, we encounter an exception. As the segment begins, the teacher notes *forget* as the complement of the verb *help* in the sentence 'He wants to help her forget,' as opposed to 'He wants to help her <u>to</u> forget.' We notice the micro-pause in line 02 as a possible indication that the teacher might have noticed something unusual about what he just said.

(9a) help her forget [Boblett, 2018; simplified]
```
01    TC:      'forget' is a complement.
02             (.)
03             yeah. looks at smartboard and back to SS
04             (0.2)
05             there's no 'to'∷ (.)↓yeah there's no 'to'∷
06             (0.5)
07             ↓yeah (.) and [there is no 'TO'∷
                             [cocks head, gaze upward
08             [(0.5)
              [scratches head, then chin
09             [looks down at floor, smiles]
10    ST:      [        why.         ]=
11    SS:      =[    light laughter    ]
```

Note first the lingering: the micro-pauses (lines 02 & 04), and the mere looking following *yeah* in line 03. Then, instead of launching into a lecture of how certain verbs can be used without the infinitive *to*, the teacher simply notices this strange phenomenon of *there's no 'to'* (lines 05 & 07) and begins to do all sorts of 'wondering' through the repetition of his noticing, the silence, the thinking gaze and gestures, as well as the 'mysterious' smile (lines 05–09), thereby creating an environment where open exploration can happen. Indeed, it is the student, not the teacher, who asks the *why* in line 10, which is immediately followed by light laughter from the other students—an initial display of interest or intrigue and a good starting point for exploration. What we see below is how the teacher's exploratory posture creates an opening for at least one student's own exploration.

(9b) help her forget [Boblett, 2018; simplified]
```
12    TC:      =[ looks down, smiling]
13             steps over to desk, smiling, looking down
14             [lifts gaze to ST1, holds]
15    ST1:     [    it's like (.) eh    ] 'make' eh: (.) it's like 'ma:ke' eh
16             (.) [        'get'        ] (0.2) n- no not 'get'=
17    TC:      [    nods vigorously   ]
```

18   ST1:   =but it's like 'make' 'let' and 'have' yeah?
19   TC: yeah (.) yeah it's like yeah. it's like '<u>ma::ke</u>'. (.)

In lines 12–14, in response to the student's *why*, the teacher remains in his 'thinking zone' (Boblett, 2018, p. 266). Rather than answering the question himself, he lifts his gaze up to ST1 and holds, at which point the latter volunteers his attempt at answering the why question (lines 15, 16, & 18). Rather than providing a straightforward 'because...' type of answer, the student launches his own exploration by drawing analogies to other similar types of verbs. Note also that his speech features a great deal of the 'imperfections' that are hallmarks of exploratory talk (e.g., pauses, cut-offs) as ST1 revises his thoughts as he goes (e.g., *no not 'get'*). As shown, ST1's exploratory response is supported by the teacher through both non-verbal (line 17) and verbal (line 19) means. At the same time, we also see below how the teacher subtly extends his invitation to explore by shifting his gaze towards the whole class as he repeats ST1's analogy (Waring & Carpenter, 2019).

(9c) help her forget [Boblett, 2018; simplified]
19   TC: [yeah (.) yeah it's like yeah. it's like '<u>ma::ke</u>'. (.)
               [*gaze shift to SS*
20   yeah we can think of it as like 'make'.
21   ST1:   for example (.) eh::: (.) he makes me cry.
22   ST?:   yeah (.) hehe
23   ST?   HEH HEH [HEH HEH HEH HEH]
24   TC: [yeah   heh   heh   heh] <u>do</u> I? °heh°=
25   SS: =ha ha ha

As can be seen, at this point, not only does ST1 proceed by offering an example sentence (line 21), but the other students also chime in with *yeah* and laughter (lines 22 & 23). The sequence ends on a jocular tone as the class reacts to the teacher's playful uptake (lines 24 & 25).

We notice that if the teacher had assumed 'the role of information provider' (Fagan, 2012) in this case, the student would have missed the opportunity to display and explore his understanding of this particular grammatical feature, i.e., certain verbs are followed by a complement without the infinitive 'to.' The teacher employs a range of slow-motion practices such as silence, elongation, repetition along with various thinking gestures. In so doing, he avoids putting the students on the spot or under any pressure to perform (as a question would most definitely do), but rather, creates an environment where the students are free to engage in various kinds of try-outs—including the risky move of joking. Indeed, it is a student who vocalizes the *why* (line 10), it is a student who tries to solve the puzzle by offering the potentially comparable cases of *make, get, let,* and *have* (lines 15, 16, & 18), and it is a student who volunteers the joking rendition of *he makes me cry* (line 21).

Welcome student initiations

Recall the case earlier where the teacher says *I want to make the story short* when a student goes beyond what is being asked for in reporting on the inventor Thomas Edison. The same student in the segment below bids for an opportunity to *comment* as the teacher finishes summarizing the meaning of 're-enact' and is about to give instructions for the upcoming re-enactment activity. At this point, the teacher could have easily said 'We need to move on.' Instead, we see her open up the space with a quick, unhedged, and welcoming go-ahead *yeah* (line 06).

(10) don't know if I can comment [Waring, 2011, p. 205]
```
01    TC:     (summarizing meaning of re-enact)
02            and they act out things like HISTORical events.
03            °what happened.°=
04    ST:     =>yeah actually I don't know if- I just-< °I don't
05            know if I can comment.°
06    TC:     >y↑eah.<
07    ST:     >yeah.< a:::::nd there're some channel see
08            eh it's u:h the public channel television?
09    TC:     mm hm?
```

Here, we see the student proceed with her comment in lines 07 & 08 by setting the scene with *public channel television* (line 08), and the teacher display her understanding, with the continuer mm hm? (line 09), that more is to come.

In addition to making space for uninvited student contribution, another welcoming gesture is spotlighting student talk as it emerges, as shown in the next extract. A student is sharing the result of their group discussion on why native speakers are difficult to understand. Notice how the teacher zooms in onto a single word that the student produces—*swallow*.

(11a) swallow [Boblett, 2020; simplified]
```
01    ST:      we talked about (0.5) uh your question,
02             u::[:h]
03    TC:         [ye][s. ]
04    ST:            [w]e decided actually (.) uh if uh- you listen to
05             native speaker, native speaker (.) can swallow some words.
06    TC:      [>do you all you have< right.
             [index finger up, shifts gaze to group
07           [he just used an interesting verb that maybe: you don't know.
             [points to ST with gaze to group
08             (0.5)
```

Line 06 is a juncture where the teacher can evaluate, accept, or simply express interest in the students' observation that native speakers can swallow some words. Instead, she shifts her gaze to the group with her index finger up, calling everyone's attention to the interesting verb that *he*, while pointing to him, *just used* (lines 06 & 07). As such, she treats what ST just said as something worthy of attention and worth waiting for. What ST uttered in passing is now staged for the larger audience to appreciate. The student is then coaxed into performing his expertise for the group as the teacher asks him to *say it again, spell it for us,* and *do it for us* (not shown).

In the final segment of this extract, the student is invited back for an encore of what he originally produced, given its merit of being very descriptive (lines 42 and 43).

(11b) swallow [Boblett, 2020; simplified]
(lines omitted)
```
40    TC:      yeah. right. so this closes up.
41             (0.8)
42             you can't swallow. [and w- tell us >that sentence again.
                                 [releases one hand to point to ST
43             because that was very descriptive what you did.
44             that was< nicely: expressed.
45    ST:      °(what part?)°
46    TC:      your- what you >said about-< what did you say about swallow.
```

Throughout the extract, the teacher builds, turn-by-turn, a platform for the student to 'glow and shine,' and in so doing, signals to the rest of the class that they are being treated, even as language learners, as people with important things to say and that this classroom is a safe and welcoming place to say them.

Our final example is of how teachers can appreciate student talk by simply showing their enjoyment of what students add to the conversation. This extract takes place in the bilingual kindergarten class that is probably familiar to you by now. (As before, the extract has been translated from French for ease of reading.) We will see two teachers (TC1 and TC2) use a variety of means to express surprise and appreciation, e.g., tone, loudness, and even what linguists call discourse markers, such as 'oh' or 'wow.' In the excerpt below, the teachers and their students are sitting in a circle on the floor. TC1 is trying to get everyone's attention before she moves on in her lesson. Just before the excerpt begins, she has announced that she wants to see 14 eyes looking at her. Notice how ST1 responds in line 01.

(12) how many eyes [Creider, 2016, p. 118]

```
01   ST1:    [no. because [Inès isn't here [and David ( )
              [gaze ahead [gaze at M      [nods towards D
02   TC1:    [ah::
03            [touches [hand to head
04   TC2:           [smiling
05   TC1:    chec[kmark gesture in front of body, towards ST1
06   ST1:         [checkmark gesture in front of body, towards TC1, smiling
07   TC1:    ohhoho![:::
08   ST?:           [and Olivier.
09   ST1:           [hands to hips
10   TC1:    when I s[ee:
11   TC2:           [that's not bad!
```

We see the two teachers work together to show their appreciation of their student's correction in multiple ways. First, TC1 says *ah*, elongating the word, while she touches her head, as if to appreciate ST1's thinking process, as TC2 smiles. TC1 then makes a check mark, as if checking off a right answer, in front of her body, facing her student, which the student offers in return. As she makes the gesture, TC1 says *ohohoho!*—which seems to be an enthusiastic way of showing surprise and pleasure. Although we do not show the rest of this exchange, we note that the student continues to participate eagerly. She joins in an exploration of the math problem at hand and finally announces, on behalf of the teacher, how many eyes *we* want to see.

Appreciate student mistakes

Finally, one potentially surprising way of being open relates to how we respond to student mistakes. Even though righting the wrong necessarily suggests the image of 'closing in' as opposed to opening up, it is possible to maintain an environment where mistakes are celebrated without being ignored. In the following segment, the teacher (TC) is quizzing the class on a list of acronyms, including *MIA* (line 01). Notice how a student's (ST) incorrect response in line 02 is taken up by the teacher.

(13a) missing in Alaska [Fagan, 2015a; modified]
```
01    TC:            <M. (.) I. (.) A.>
02    ST:            missing (.) in (0.2) Alaska.
03                   [(0.4)
                     [TC looks towards ST
04    TC:   →        $mis[sing in Alaska.$ ]
05    SS:                [hehehehehehehe]hehe
06    TC:   →        that's really- that's really cute.
07                   [(2.0)
                     [TC smiles and shakes her head
```

We begin by observing what could have been done upon the production of the student's mistaken interpretation of *MIA*. Typical measures widely observed in practice and extensively studied are recasts (i.e., providing the correct alternative, e.g., *missing in action*) and various types of prompts that provide clues to what the problem or the correct version might be (e.g., *Missing in...?*) (Lyster, Saito, & Sato, 2013). Notably, in this case, the teacher does neither.

Instead, we see her shift her gaze to the student, getting into the position to address her next bit of her talk directly to the student (line 03). She then, in line 04, repeats the student's response in a smiley voice, just a beat before the class bursts into laughter (line 05), thus matching the class's jocular uptake of the different interpretation of MIA. This is followed by the personalized compliment *that's really cute* (line 06), which entirely sidesteps the issue of correctness. She then takes a full (2.0) second to savor the student's response as she smiles and shakes her head. Thus, **welcoming** is done by taking the time to appreciate what the student has offered so far. As the segment continues, we see the teacher take a step further to validate the student's response. (Transcription notes: $ = smiley voice, ° = quiet voice.)

(13b) missing in Alaska [Fagan, 2015a; modified]
08   TC $we could say that.[$ that could be the new MIA.=
                         [*to ST*

09   ST: = °yeah.°
10   TC: MI↑A. missing in Alaska. °$it could be.$°
11   [(0.8)
                [*TE smiles at all SS*
12   [°that's very creative. I like that.° but it's missing in action.
                [*to ST*
13   [(1.0)
14   [*SS write it down*

In line 08, the teacher proceeds, in a smiley voice, not to reject the student's interpretation, but to accept it as a possibility. She then shifts her gaze to the rest of the class as she announces its potential as the *new MIA*, thus making her acceptance even more public. Then in line 10, she repeats for the second time the student's interpretation and her own good-humored acceptance in a smiley voice. During the (0.8) second gap in line 11, she smiles at all the students rather than making any next move. In line 12, she shifts her gaze back to the student and offers a second personalized compliment *that's very creative* and explicitly states her personal liking in a quiet voice before offering the correction *but it's missing in action*.

What we notice here is a tremendous amount of lingering and savoring (as opposed to glossing over and fixing) of the student's *cute* and *creative* interpretation of MIA. By engaging these personalized compliments along with the explicit claim of *I like*, the teacher's response can be heard as not driven by a narrow focus on the correct answer but as featuring a genuinely personal appreciation (Fagan, 2015a) for the student's ingenuity. One might argue that it is precisely this openness to mistakes that invites the student to take the risk of offering *missing in Alaska* as a possibility in the first place. Put otherwise, treating a student's incorrect answer as such, the teacher makes it evident that this class is an open space where even **mistakes are appreciated** in their own right.

In sum, there is no doubt that being open is an important element in fostering an inviting environment where students are given the space to explore, to flounder, and to shine. And as shown above (although not an exhaustive list), such openness may be created by engaging in exploratory talk, welcoming student contributions, and appreciating student mistakes. One larger theme that appears to be emerging, again, is the importance of not rushing to move on, but taking the time to work with a problem or appreciate student contributions on their own terms and in all of their dimensions beyond correctness. Taking the time to savor the moment, in other words, plays a sizable role in fostering an open environment that is inviting.

Resources for Being Open

(1) make observations of learner talk (e.g., *He just used an interesting word*)
(2) say 'yes', not 'no' (e.g., to uninvited student contributions)
(3) linger (e.g., silence, smile, repetition, slower pace, mutual gaze, thinking gestures, self-talk, puzzled observation)
(4) stage student performance (e.g., index finger up, gaze shift to class; *can you do X for us?*)
(5) use personalized compliments (e.g., *that's very creative*)
(6) use tone, gesture, and markers of enjoyment (e.g., *a::h*)

Changing

So far, we have shown what is there to be noticed in being open and what kinds of specific verbal and visible resources may be used to carry out the relevant conduct. While noticing serves as a prerequisite, and sets the stage, for changing, it does not automatically lead to change. A key component in our cycle of micro-reflection entails the work of instigating changes in one's conduct, and such work, we argue, must be reflective in nature. As such, we offer a series of guided exercises to facilitate this intrinsically reflective process of changing that moves from what to look for, to what to think about, and finally, to what to do.

What to look for

1. Based on your experiences as a student, a teacher, or an observer, what would you say might be three signs of an open classroom? More specifically, what would be some of the features of the student conduct? What would be some of the features of the teacher conduct? You can write your thoughts below.

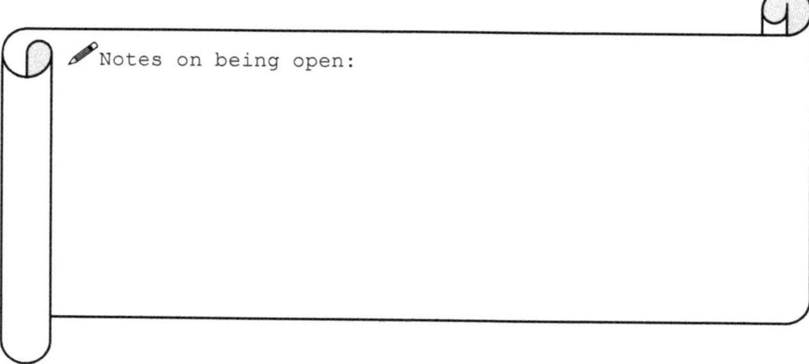

2. Take a look at the following two extracts (one repeated from above). What are the observable signs of a classroom moment being open or not open? (Transcription note: empty parentheses = talk that cannot be heard for transcription.)

(14) no questions [Waring data]
01   [(0.5)
           [*TC approaches ST1 and ST2*
02   TC: [do you have any questions?
           [*to ST1*
03   ST1: no.
04   TC: [very clear?
           [*to S2*
05   ST2: yes.

(15) homeless people [Waring data]
01   TC: okay. homeless people are not as polite a:s (0.2) <u>teachers</u>.
02   (5.0)
03   >ST1, go ahead.<
04   (1.0)
05   ST1: yeah.
06   (0.8)
07   someti:mes (.) u:h homeless people (0.5) u:h are <u>al</u>so (.)
08   <u>p</u>olite.
09   (2.0)
10   <u>b</u>ut, in general, (0.8) u:h we can say in general °homeless
11   people° <u>e</u>veryday uh- uh- uh- uh- the::y uh- not- not-enjoy
12   uh- their li:fe.
13   (0.5)
14   so:, (0.2) uh- uh- in <u>gen</u>eral, homeless people are happy, so
15   have no uh: uh: uh no: *gesture of effort and helplessness*
16   SS: huhhuhuuhhh
17   ST1: <u>any</u>[way,
18   SS: [hehehhe
19   TC: [>no keep going keep going.
20   [they have they have no:::]
           [*inducing gesture*
21   ST1: [(   )] can't can't po- can't be <u>po</u>lite.
22   TC: *nods*

```
23   ST1:   compared to (0.2) teachers, to::::: (0.2) friend, (0.2) u:h to
24          be poli:te (.) student.
25          (1.0)
26          that my opi(hh)nion b(hh)[ut
27   SS:                             [heheheheheh
28   ST1:   ju:st to: justify points to board °the sentence.°
29   TC:    °who disagrees with the sentence.°
30          (0.2)
31          go ahead.
32   ST2:   u:h homeless people usually sit or sleep they don't
33          (       ) but uh (.) teacher, we: have some more
34          (relationship) so
35          we can say hi hi, but (0.5) homeless people (.) u:::m (0.2)
36          they don't (interact) a lot we don(hhh)'t kn(hhh)ow
37          we have no idea (   [    )]
38   ST1:                       [(    )]
39   TC:    [>okay,<
        [to ST1
40   ST1:   you have no: relation with homeless people,
41          everyday ( )
42          and the:y ask you to give some (.) money uh: to (.) pay
43          attention, to them.
44          (0.2)
45          so you: ( ) relation, with (.) when ( ) so, you can ( )
46          they are (.)
47          polite, (.) or not.
48          (2.0)
49   ST3:   I think that [hom-
50   ST4:                [( )
51   ST3:   [sorry
        [gestures for the other to continue
52   ST4:   ( ) they ask something ( ), they would say (continues)
```

What to think about

1. In our noticing section above, we have drawn attention to some practices of
    not being open and of being open. The lists are most definitely not exhaus-
    tive. Take a moment to focus on the idea of being open and think of any
    other practices (positive or negative) based on your experiences and/or

observations as a teacher or a student. Be as specific as possible in your description of the practice.

(a) When is it done (e.g., initiating or responsive position), how is it done, and what response(s) does it receive?

(b) What words, gestures, intonation, and timing are used in its delivery?

(c) What alternatives are available at the time of its production?

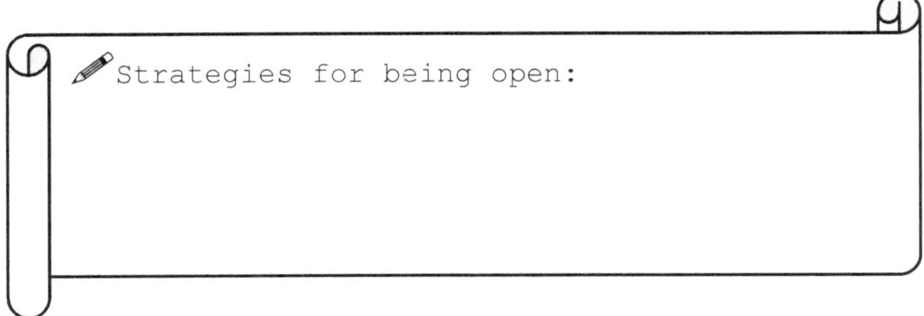

2. In the example of being open discussed earlier and reproduced below, for each turn set in bold type, consider the following:

(a) what the teacher could be doing at this particular juncture but is not;

(b) what she does instead;

(c) what interactional resources (verbal and visible) she uses to do what she does;

(d) in what way her choices might be opening up a space for student participation;

(e) how her conduct is received by the students;

(f) what other choices there might be at this juncture to promote openness.

(16) swallow [Boblett, 2020; simplified]

```
01  ST:     we talked about (0.5) uh your question,
02          u::[:h]
03  TC:        [ye][s.]
04  ST:             [w]e decided actually (.) uh if uh- you listen to
05          native speaker, native speaker (.) can swallow some words.
06  TC:     [>do you all you have <right.
            [index finger up, shifts gaze to group
07          [he just used an interesting verb that maybe: you don't
            [points to ST with gaze to group
08          know.
09          (0.5)
```

10   [s̲ay it agai̲n.
            [*minimal point and gaze to ST*
11 ST: [°swallow.°]
12 TC: [*stands up*]
13   y̲es. [can you spell it for us?
            [*goes to board*
14 ST: S, W, (0.8) A, L, L, (0.8) O, >W.<
(lines omitted)
24 TC: ok, so, what i̲s [swallow. can you do it for us? physically?
            [*turns to ST*
25 ST: [°t̲his.°
            [*demonstrates swallows with hand on neck*
(lines omitted)
40 TC: y̲eah. r̲ight. so this closes up.
41   (0.8)
42   you can't swallow. [and w- tell us >that sentence again.
                        [*releases one hand to point to ST*
43   because that was very descriptive what you did.
44   that was< nicely: expressed.
45 ST: °(what part?)°
46 TC: your- what you >said about<
47   w̲hat did you [say about swallow
                        [*gestures to board*

What to do

1. Based on the skills you have developed so far, observe an actual lesson (with a video-camera if possible) with a specific focus on strategies for (not) being open. Organize your notes using the following table.

2. Repeat the same exercise above with a video-recording of your own teaching, and invite a colleague to either join the exercise or offer feedback on your own analysis.

3. With the observational materials you have now gathered (video recordings preferably), identify moments where the class manifests a sense of being open, and try to work backwards to figure out what has been done to lead to that moment.

4. Try out specific strategies for being open in your own class one at a time. Make note of its effect in terms of specific student conduct. Make adjustments accordingly as you repeat the exercise.

Strategies for being open	
Strategies	Details
1.	(a) What could have been done differently at this particular moment in the interaction?
2.	
3.	(b) What is not being done, and why?
	(c) What exactly is being done, and how?
	(d) How is what is being done taken up by the participants in the data?

Strategies for not being open	
Strategies	Details
1.	(a) What could have been done differently at this particular moment in the interaction?
2.	
3.	(b) What is not being done, and why?
	(c) What exactly is being done, and how?
	(d) How is what is being done taken up by the participants in the data?

BEING EQUAL

Finally, fostering an inviting environment involves what we have come to call being equal. Admittedly, teacher and student are not equal participants in a pedagogical interaction, with one being more knowledgeable about certain specific content (e.g., language) than the other. Interaction, however, can be structured so as to feature what van Lier (1996) calls 'symmetry'—'equal participation rights and duties' (p. 14)—so that all parties can share the rights and duties of, for example, question-askers and answer-givers. In addition, students can be seen as people with expertise from outside the classroom that can be valuable inside the classroom. How to achieve this symmetry is our focus for this section. Here again, we follow our cycle of micro-reflection with the aim of developing the ability to see and then to exercise being equal, moving from noticing to changing.

Noticing

The typical classroom interaction is rampant with instances of not being equal, as most of the time the teacher is the person who asks questions, gives directions, selects the next speaker, and produces evaluations. Being equal would then involve engaging in counter-intuitive, 'non-classroom-like' strategies. In this section, we will work through noticing two such teacher strategies.

> **Strategies for being equal**: (1) position self as co-learner; (2) position other as independent agent.

Position self as co-learner

We present two examples below: first from a graduate writing tutoring session and then from a French-immersion kindergarten classroom. In the segment from the graduate writing center, we invite you to notice the tutor's (TR) shift into a position of a co-learner with the tutee (TT). In lines 01–09, we see the tutor launching a critique of the circular problem in the tutee's writing and the tutee displaying her understanding of that critique.

(17a) what do you do [Waring, 2016]
```
01    TR:    (lines omitted) the writing is a little bit circular .hh you talk
02           about A: and B: and you go back to A a little agai:n< and kind've-
03    TT:    °'kay.°=
04    TR:    =they're not as linear as (.) it- could be.
05           (5.0)
06    TT:    .hh so basically I'm watching out for like
07           am I following that line- of thought-
08    TR:    ri:ght.
09    TT:    right throu:gh without- (0.4) bringing in something else? °okay.°
```

What the tutor does next is offer a suggestion, but she does so in such a way that positions herself as a co-learner who admires a friend's writing and benefits from learning her tactic (line 11):

(17b) what do you do [Waring, 2016]
```
09    TT:    right throu:gh without- (0.4) brin[ging in] something else? °okay.°
10    TR:                                      [ri:ght. ]
11           a friend of mine has this great (0.2) tactic.
12    TT:    °what does she do.°
13    TR:    she uses this to- to write cuz I ↑love her ↑writing.
14    TT:    aha?
15    TR:    an' >I always say what do you ↑do what do you do =
16    TT:      [>right right.<]
17    TR:    =[ and I started ]to use it recently I think it ↑really ↑works.< =
18           .hh each time she begins a paragraph,
```

19	TT:	[yeah.]
20	TR:	[she-] she asks a <u>que</u>stion.
21		(0.8)
22		u:m >↓she says this is the question I'm going to answer in this
23		paragraph. .hh and she (0.2) <u>wri</u>tes that paragraph.<
24	TT:	an' then she gets [rid of]the question.
25	TR:	[she ge-]
26		**gets rid of the qu(h)estion! (continues)**

As can be seen, instead of proceeding with a direct suggestion (e.g., answer a specific question for each paragraph), TR offers a story in which she is self-positioned as a learner seeking writing advice from a friend whose writing she admires (lines 11, 13, 15, 17–18, 22–23, 25–26). Note that she takes on the voice of an admirer (*great tactic...I love her writing*) (lines 11 & 13) and an eager advice seeker (*what do you do what do you do* in line 15)—as someone who is learning to write as well, just like the tutee. At the same time, we also observe the tutee following the telling, as a co-learner, with great interest throughout the sequence. For example, she asks a question to forward the telling in line 12, she says *aha* to get TR to continue in line 14 (also see line 19), in line 16 she produces *right right* in quick pace and in overlap immediately after TR's self-reported speech of seeking advice, and she collaboratively completes the tutor's telling in line 24.

In the next segment from the kindergarten classroom, the teacher (TC) is helping a student say the date (including the day of the week) in French. In line 01, we see the teacher begin to sing a song about the days of the week in French starting with *Monday*. We then see ST1 take the cue and continue with *mardi* (for Tuesday) in line 02, which the teacher acknowledges in line 03 both with a repetition and by pointing at the calendar. For readability, an English translation of the transcript is presented below, with the exception of the two key French words: *mardi* = Tuesday; *mars* = March. See if you can notice a shift happening in line 05, where TC moves out of a typical teacher position.

(18a) mars and mardi [Creider, 2016]

01	TC:	m:::::: [Monday,] m:
		[*singing voice *]
02	ST1:	[*mouths 'Monday'*]
03		°mardi.°
04	TC:	mardi. *points at calendar*
05		↑oh. *looks at calendar* mars and (.) mardi (0.6) start (.) with (.)
06	ST2:	↑ma:r.
07	TC:	*looks at ST2* ↑ma:r.

In line 05, TC produces *oh* in raised pitch to indicate surprise and realization (Bolden, 2006, p. 63), sounding like someone in the process of learning something new. She then takes a moment to simply look at the source of this new information—the calendar where *mars* and *mardi* are written. This is followed by saying aloud the two words that constitute the focus of her developing understanding while still looking at the calendar. Note that her delivery is punctuated with pauses (after *and* and then *mardi*) that embody a process of trying to figure something out. Thereafter, she begins to voice the point of her realization—that there is something notable about what the two words *start with*. Without completing the utterance, this noticing is also produced slowly with micro-pauses after each word, again as if she were thinking through the new discovery. In line 06, we see ST2 join this process of discovery by completing the teacher's utterance with the 'punchline' of the latter's noticing—with raised pitch and elongation that indicate pride and success.

Notably, what the teacher does in line 05 is not leading an activity (as she does in line 01), providing an answer, or assessing a response (as she does in line 04). Instead, she does a lot of work voicing her own struggle as a co-learner through exploratory talk (see above) in lieu of, for example, asking 'Who can tell me what these words have in common?' or 'I'd like everyone to notice that both of these words start with the same sound.' This self-positioning as a co-learner is a stance embraced and validated by ST2 as the latter chimes in as a collaborator in identifying what is noticeable about the two words, which the teacher accepts with a repetition in matching prosody as she turns to ST2 (line 07).

As the segment continues, we see further evidence that the students appear to take the shift in the teacher's position as a cue for joining in as collaborators in this learning. But first, notice that the teacher lets a (0.4) second of silence pass (line 08), as these micro-moments of simple silence seem to be integral to the process of learning. She then takes the marker (line 09) as she prepares to write, picking up a writing instrument being part and parcel of one's process of working out a problem. This is followed by a move from the two individual words to a broader statement of *there are a lot of words that start with*, shifting from specific instances to larger patterns being another crucial component of learning. Note that she pauses after *with* and makes a gesture (line 10) that solicits help from the students. In other words, she is not just doing learning, but also doing, more specifically, co-learning.

(18b) mars and mardi [Creider, 2016]
08   (0.4)
09   TC: *takes marker* **there are lots of words that start with** (0.2)
10   *throws hand out to the side*

11   ST3:   li[ke MA::rs.]
12   TC: [ma:::r   ]>yes. good.< *points towards calendar* in French.
13   [mars,
               [*pen towards word mars*
14   [mardi
               [*pen towards word mardi*
15   ST4:   and Thursday.

As can be seen, ST3 offers another word (albeit in English) that starts with *mar* (line 11), and S4 continues with another date of the week in line 15.

Overall, the verbal resources used by the teacher in this particular instance to position herself as a co-learner include *oh* in raised pitch, slow repetitions of key terms with pauses, incomplete utterances that index thinking, and movement beyond individual exemplars of the phenomenon. 'Oh,' for example, has been documented in the conversation analytic literature as a practice for indicating a change-of-state (Heritage, 1984). The visible resources, on the other hand, involve looking and thinking in silence, gesturing to elicit help, picking up a writing instrument to facilitate problem solving, and pointing to accompany the repetition of key terms.

In both cases above, we see the teacher and the tutor in their own ways shift from the canonical position of the knower to that of a not-yet-knowing participant, and we see how that shift engages and invites co-participation in a journey of learning.

Position other as independent agent

While position self as co-learner achieves being equal through a claim of co-membership (Erickson, 1975), being equal may also be accomplished through positioning others as individuals with their independent goals, plans, and preferences. The former emphasizes sameness, and the latter features separateness or autonomy. We show two examples below from post-observation conferences after a mentor has observed a mentee's class, where we can notice evidence of the mentor (MR) treating the mentee (ME) as an independent agent. The first example involves what the mentor considers to be an issue of timing with regard to a particular reading activity handled by the mentee. As the segment begins, the mentor is finishing making the observation that having students write down answers to questions as they read can take a while (lines 01 & 02), with which the mentee wholeheartedly agrees (lines 03–05). The two solidify their agreement in lines 06 & 07. Notice the specific way in which the mentor begins to frame her suggestion in line 08.

(19) speed this up [Waring, 2016]
```
01   MR:    cuz when they have to write answers to the questions?
02          that usually takes them [a while.]
03   ME:                           [exactly. ] they- they- that was taking them
04          longer. u:m, >becuz I was< going around? they- they read? (.) the
05          whole thing? bu:t writing it down was: [taking a lot of time.]
06   MR:                                          [ right. right. right.  ]
                                                  [nods
07   ME:    [yeah.
            [nods
08   MR:    so::, um (.) if you wanna speed this up,
09   ME:    [mm hm,]
            [nods
10   MR:    [  u:m,  ] (0.8) you can (.) have them (.) not write it down.
11   ME:    mm hm,
(lines omitted addressed to outside noise)
12   MR:    °okay.° u:m, or? you can do ski↑mming? where you ask them
13          the wh- questions?=
14   ME:    =okay.
```

As can be seen, nowhere throughout this interaction does MR explicitly treat the timing as a problem. Instead, she simply observes the time-consuming nature of the activity, which also allows ME to respond as an equal by offering like-minded agreement (lines 03–05; 07), rather than accepting or acquiescing. After reaching a common understanding regarding the nature of the activity, in line 08, what MR does is notably not advising ME to change her practice or improve her timing. Instead, she offers *speed this up* as an option for ME to consider, and should the latter make that decision, *skimming* as a course of action to implement that decision (line 12). In other words, ME is positioned as someone who has the ultimate say in her decisions as a growing professional.

Our second example also comes from a post-observation conference, where the concern involves having only one student in the class just observed.

(20) put you off your game [Waring, 2016]
```
01   MR:    a:nd, (0.2) you were telling me a little bit earlier about
02          having that one student.
03          (0.2)
04          do you f↑ee:l tha:t (.) that sort of (.) put you off of your game,
```

05		>starting off the class with that, [or d'y feel-]<,=
06	ME:	[a̲ little bit].
07	MR:	=y[eah],
08	ME:	[yeah].
09	MR:	>well t̲ell me about it.<
10	ME:	well I think (.) that (.) y'know I had tried to think of contingencies for
11		various things,

In line 01, MR uses *you were telling me about X*, where ME is positioned as someone taking the initiative to notice the problem. Then in line 03, MR lets a brief (0.2) second of silence pass, where a bit of space is created for ME to expand upon what she herself talked about *a little bit earlier*. In lines 04 & 05, MR uses *do you feel...*—a formulation that shows his effort to understand the situation from ME's perspective (as opposed to 'What do you feel?'). We also see pauses as well as the hedging *sort of*, both of which convey a tone of exploration as MR explores ME's perspectives, which in turn invites and inspires ME to explore her own thinking and feeling, as she does later (lines 10 & 11). Finally, the phrase *put you off your game* is carefully crafted to position ME as a professional with a game plan that can materialize with various degrees of success, as is the case for all professionals.

In other words, rather than problematizing the low attendance, exploring its reasons, or perhaps more relevantly, critiquing the teacher's handling of the one-person classroom, the mentor frames it as a practical problem and expresses interest in hearing the mentee's experience of being confronted with that problem. This positioning work appears to be instrumental, as noted above, in creating a space for the mentee to articulate her thoughts as a professional (lines 10 & 11).

As can be seen, the mentor makes a number of moves to position the mentee as an independent agent or to put her in the driver's seat, so to speak, with phrasing such as *You were telling me a little bit about X, Do you feel that ... put you off your game*. He also pauses and hedges to create an inviting space for independent thoughts. As evidenced in this dialog, these moves are effective in getting the mentee and the mentor on the same page and are conducive to the mentee's subsequent reflection.

In sum, one path towards fostering an inviting environment is to achieve being equal, which can be accomplished with **position self as co-learner** and **position other as independent agent**. By shifting the assumption that students, tutees, and mentees are automatically deficient, these strategies treat them as equals of their teachers, tutors, and mentors in the larger endeavor of academic advancement and professional growth. We summarize the resources for how exactly this can be accomplished below.

Resources for Being Equal

(1) share story of own learning (e.g., *A friend of mine has this great tactic*)
(2) publicly embody the process of learning (e.g., slow down, pause, hedge, repeat, write, leave utterances incomplete, and say *oh* to convey spontaneous realization)
(3) observe, not problematize (e.g., *X takes time* or *You were telling me X*)
(4) offer up possibilities for consideration, not direct or advise (e.g., *if you want to do X*)
(5) show curiosity about the other's perspective (e.g., *did you feel that you were off your game…*)

Changing

So far, we have focused on noticing what types of teacher conduct are conducive to being equal, and what interactional resources (verbal and visible) can be recruited to assemble such conduct. To move from noticing to changing, we now offer a series of guided exercises to facilitate this transition.

What to look for

1. Based on your experiences as a student, a teacher, or an observer, what would you say might be three signs of an equal classroom? More specifically, what would be some of the features of the student conduct? What would be some of the features of the teacher conduct? You can write your notes here:

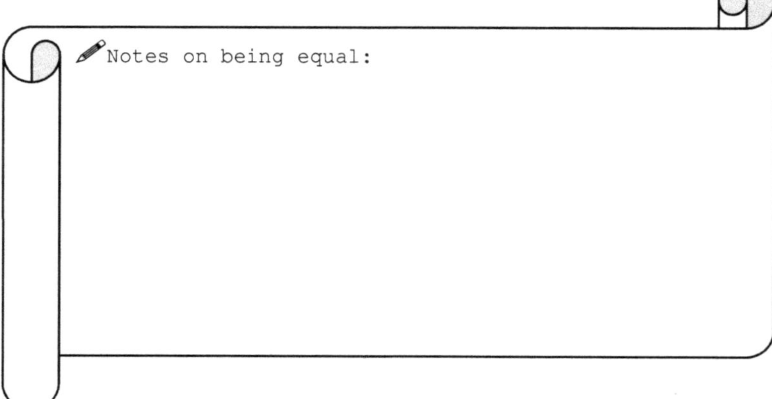

2. Consider the following extract, where the class is doing a grammar exercise in their textbook where they use prompts to complete sentences with the present progressive. What are the observable signs of a classroom moment being 'equal' or 'not equal'?

(21) poetry [Waring, 2009, pp. 505–506]
01   ST: [I don't believe it. I didn't know your sister wrote poet.
            [*reads*
02   (0.5)
03   TC: poetry.
04   ST: poetry. how long your sister (.) has been writing poetry.
05   *looks up at T*
06   TC: °oka:::y, let's write this d↑own.°
(lines omitted)
07   how long (0.2) has she >°been writing poetry.° <=it's a
08   question.
09   (0.6)
10   ST: °a[::h.° yeah.]
11   TC: [oka y.   ]
12   (0.5)
13   °good.° number six, Yuka?

3. Consider another extract from the French immersion kindergarten classroom. Prior to the extract, one of the two teachers (TC1) mentioned seeing a polar bear on a book cover, and ST1 called out that *there's not much of them in the world*. The extract begins with TC1 referring to what ST1 has said. Again, for readability, an English translation of the transcript is presented below. What are some observable signs of any classroom moment being equal or not equal?

(22) polar bears [Creider, 2016]
01   TC1 : ST1 you said tha- there aren't many polar bears.
02   SS: *hands up*
03   ST1: °( ) into brown bears.°
04   TC1: what's that?
05   ST1: turning into <u>brown</u> bears.
06   TC2: *puzzled expression*
07   TC1: they're transformed, into bears,=
08   TC2: =this morning, I dunno what you're up to.

09		[but ehhehehe
10	ST1:	[they jump in the water and then they come up open air
11		>and they turn into brown bea[rs.<
12	ST3:	[>no they don't.

What to think about

1. In our noticing section above, we have drawn attention to some strategies
    for not being equal, such as playing a dominant role in asking questions
    and giving evaluations and for being equal, such as **positioning self as
    co-learner**. The lists are most definitely not exhaustive. Take a moment to
    focus on the idea of 'being equal' and think of any other strategies (positive
    or negative) based on your experiences and/or observations as a teacher or
    a student. Be as specific as possible in your description of the strategy.
    (a) When is it done (e.g., initiating or responsive position), how is it done,
         and what response(s) does it receive?
    (b) What words, gestures, intonation, and timing are used in its delivery?
    (c) What alternatives are available at the time of its production?

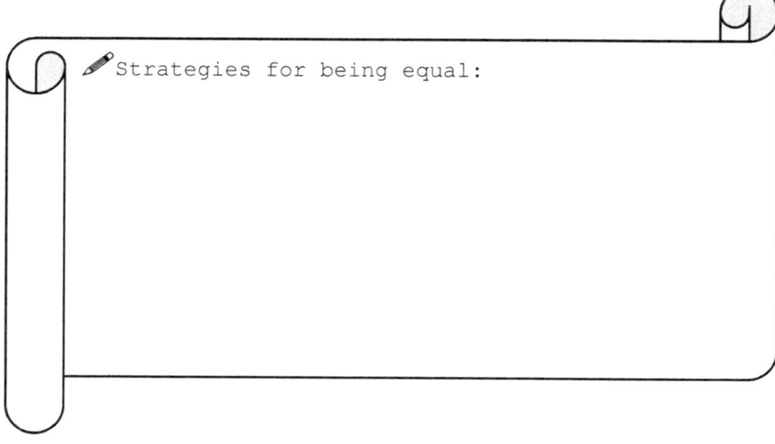

2. Consider another instance here from tutoring in a graduate school writing
    skills center between a tutor (TR) and a tutee (TT). For each turn in bold
    type, describe:
    (a) what alternatives there might be;
    (b) what the tutor does precisely (e.g., X as opposed to Y);

(c) what specific resources are used;

(d) in what way the tutor's conduct might be opening up a space for learning;

(e) how it is responded to;

(f) what other choices there might be at this juncture to promote equality.

(23) I go back and forth (Waring, 2016, p. 85]

01   TR: I- ↑I: go back and forth because >I first said

02   I'll (go a' put this) I started to read your inclusion

03   example I said they're all kind of different. So I- get

04   r̲id of it, th(h)e ↑s(h)econd time I read it I pu- I put it

05   back again< in the end I think it's b̲etter .hhh

06   TT: m̲hm̲

07   TR: so you- you u̲se community as a larger category.=

08   TT: =>I̲ think so [↑too.<

09   TR: [yea:h.

10   TT: I ag̲ree with you.=

11   TR: right?=

12   TT: =totally. [↑y̲eah ↑y̲eah. I- I [totally agree with you.

13   TR: [yeah   [so, I- I-

14   >even though< I went back and forth with it [( )

15   TT: [an'

16   I ↑wanna do that I ↑wanna synthesize I ↑wanna it to

17   be[come more-

18   TR: [yeah.

19   TT: y̲eah.

20   TR: °y̲eah°

21   TT: °'kay°

3. Here is another instance from tutoring in a graduate school writing skills center between a tutor (TR) and a tutee (TT). For the turn in bold type, describe:

(a) what the tutor could be doing at this particular juncture but is not;

(b) what she does instead;

(c) what interactional resources (verbal and visible) she uses to do what she does;

(d) in what way her choices might be creating a sense of equality;

(e) how her conduct is received by the tutee;

(f) what other choices there might be at this juncture to promote equality.

(24) don't know if you're going to buy this [Waring data]

```
01   TR:    an:::d (0.2) I think the:se are the fou::r u::::m (1.0)
02          things right? °your ide- not- ( [ )°
03   TT:                                    [commu[nity?
04   TR:                                            [°( ) ( )
05          learning ( ) learning.°
06   TT:    °( ) learning basically yeah.°
07   TR:    .hhhh
08   TT     [°and inquiry.°
09   TR     [I'M TRYING TO (0.2) I- I don't know if you're
10          going to buy this but um (.) w- we'll look at some
11          specific examples too. I'm trying to get you to put
12          inclusion into com[munity,] and power into voice.=
13   TT:                      [ okay? ]
14          =yeah. I think I can do that?=
15   TR:    =so you have three.
16   TT:    =three. yeah.
```

What to do

1. Based on the skills you have developed so far, observe an actual lesson (with a video-camera if possible) with a specific focus on strategies for (not) being equal. Organize your notes using the following table.

Strategies for being equal	
Strategies	Details
1.	(a) What could have been done differently at this particular moment
2.	in the interaction?
3.	(b) What is not being done, and why?
	(c) What exactly is being done, and how?
	(d) How is what is being done taken up by the participants in the data?

Strategies for not being equal	
Strategies	Details
1.	(a) What could have been done differently at this particular moment
2.	in the interaction?
3.	(b) What is not being done, and why?
	(c) What exactly is being done, and how?
	(d) How is what is being done taken up by the participants in the data?

2. Repeat the same exercise above with a video-recording of your own teaching, and invite a colleague to either join the exercise or offer feedback on your own analysis.

3. With the observational materials you have gathered (video recordings preferably), identify moments where the class manifests a sense of being equal, and try to work backwards to figure out what has been done to lead to that moment.

4. Try out specific strategies for being equal in your own class one at a time. Make note of each strategy's effect in terms of specific student conduct. Make adjustments accordingly as you repeat the exercise.

Chapter 3

Attend to Learner Voices

The second component of our FAB framework is attending to learner voice. It is important to note that honoring the primacy of learner voice is not new in the literature on teaching and learning and has, in fact, been well-rehearsed with such notions as student-centered learning or interest-driven pedagogy (Barron, 2006; Moll et al., 1992; Morrell, 2002; van Lier, 1996; Vygotsky, 1978). Our focus, however, revolves around how learner-centeredness, for example, can be achieved at a much more micro level (e.g., Tadic, 2019; Waring & Yu, 2016)—by being responsive to the moment on a turn-by-turn basis in conversation or invoking the 'principle of contingency' (Waring, 2016). As noted in Chapter 1, attending to learner voices requires the skill of 'Teach off your students, not at them' (Johnson & Dellagenlo, 2013, p. 432). More specifically, we think of such attending as a project sculpted from two perspectives: provide contingent assistance and build on student talk. Insofar as being attentive calls for close listening—and true hearing, it means providing assistance at the exact moment when it is needed. It also means building on student talk in such a way that demonstrates a spot-on understanding of that talk (Goodwin, 2013). For practicing teachers in their daily professional life, the challenge is how such attending can actually be done in moment-to-moment interaction. We hope to make evident this 'how' in the ensuing sections by engaging the micro-reflective cycle of noticing and changing.

PROVIDING CONTINGENT ASSISTANCE

Providing contingent assistance is easier said than done, given the centrality of lesson planning in teacher training. After all, adhering to a plan can prevent one from being contingent, and being contingent can require veering off the plan. In this section, in keeping with our cycle of micro-reflection, we first work on noticing what not providing contingent assistance looks like before demonstrating the kinds of practices for providing such assistance. Building on this foundational noticing of what providing contingent assistance entails in the specifics of interaction, we then delve into the possibilities of implementing changes—through a set of step-by-step changing exercises that focus on what to look for, what to think about, and what to do in others' and our own classes.

Noticing

Not providing contingent assistance

As will be shown, not providing contingent assistance becomes most salient when the teacher (especially novice teachers) persists with the same course of action despite the obvious failure of that action. In the following episode, the class is doing a vocabulary exercise based on a reading passage, where a set of items in one column is matched to their definitions in a separate column. In line 02, ST1 provides the correct matching between the word 'endorphins' and its definition 'chemicals that make us feel better' although (as it becomes clear later in the transcript) this is not exactly the answer the teacher (TC) is seeking. (Transcription note: empty parentheses = untranscribable talk.)

(1a) endorphins [Waring, 2015, p. 71]

```
01    TC:    okay, so from the sentence we can tell 'endorphins' mea:ns (0.8)
02    ST1:   chemicals that make us feel better.
03    TC:    okay.
04           (0.8)
05           and uh ST2 according to the sentence 'endorphins' mea:ns (1.0)
06    ST2:   °it's the same word (  ) I can't explain ( )°
```

With *from the sentence* (line 01), the teacher is in fact trying to have the students locate the meaning of 'endorphins' from a sentence in the original text, not in the column of definitions. Rather than offering a clarification in line 03, the teacher acknowledges and accepts ST1's answer and proceeds to direct the same question to ST2 in line 05, who explains, in a quiet voice, her inability to answer. Now although ST2's response cannot be made out in its entirety, what we can hear is her 'protest' of not being able to *explain* because *it's the same word* (line 06). One wonders what she means by *same word*, i.e., same as what? In any case, ST2 has expressed confusion, and providing contingent assistance would entail figuring out the nature of that confusion. What the teacher does next, however, is very different.

(1b) endorphins [Waring, 2015, p. 71]

07   TC: well- but according to the sentence,
08   if we use the (.) kind of <u>c</u>ontext to help us. This sentence
09   really tells us a<u>no</u>ther way to talk about the meaning right?
10   ST?:   °mhm°
11   (3.5)
12   TC: [<u>wh</u>at is that-]
13   ST2:   [(   )] I don't know! I can't explain in the
14   sentence. when you know the word, it's difficult to explain.

Instead of trying to find out what ST2 means by *the same*, the teacher repeats his original question, emphasizing that the *sentence* provides another way of talking about the meaning (lines 08 & 09), remaining unresponsive to the possibility that ST2 may not have a clue as to which sentence he is referring to. As the segment continues below, we see that once the reference of *the sentence* is made clear, ST2 has no trouble providing the answer. Her use of *Oh* in line 23 is particularly telling, as if she were saying, 'Oh I would have given you that minutes ago if I'd known what you'd been talking about!'

(1c) endorphins [Waring, 2015, p. 71]

15   TC: I:: don't think it's difficult. if you take a look at li:ne which line is it.
(lines omitted)
20   TE: so according to lines 10 and 11- I don't want you
21   to give any- you don't <u>h</u>ave to think of any (.) new idea. I'm asking what
22   does the story say.
23   ST2:   oh. it's natural painkiller.
24   TE: exactly. yeah. (continues)

There are countless ways in which we as teachers experience moments of staunch persistence, where we act single-mindedly, rather than *inter*act with the human beings in front of us. What does providing contingent assistance look like then? It might be helpful to note up front that the key word here is 'contingent.' Contingent assistance is not any assistance. For instance, it's not the 'big picture' assistance that you plan in advance, which is valuable in its own right (e.g., my students need help with third-person singular). It's the kind of assistance that happens in the micro-moments of classroom interaction—directly in response to what is going on *now*, or more precisely, what someone has *just* said or done—as in the last 10th of a second, for example. In what follows, we can notice three possible ways in which this can happen, this kind of noticing being a key component of micro-reflection.

> **Strategies for providing contingent assistance**: (1) offer before the 'ask'; (2) adjust as it goes; (3) assist anyway.

Offer before the 'ask'

How do we know our students need help? We know for sure, of course, when they explicitly ask for help, which doesn't happen very often, given the constraints of classroom discourse that often places students in the R slot of the IRF (initiation-response-feedback) structure. Moreover, as language learners, students are not always fully capable of articulating the nature of their problems, which are often up to the teacher to diagnose and formulate. The student who had trouble responding to the teacher's request regarding 'endorphins' in the prior excerpt, for example, was only able to convey her confusion in such vague terms as *it's the same*. In these moments, the teacher's ability as a 'detective' or 'mind-reader' would be of utmost value. Ideally, assistance should be dispatched before it is explicitly requested, and this timeliness is what renders such assistance contingent. The following excerpt is taken from an adult ESL class, where the students have just worked in pairs to find something different or special about their partners, and ST1 is now sharing her finding about ST2 with the whole class. Let's see if we can notice how and when exactly the teacher offers her assistance.

(2) scholarship [Boblett, 2020]
```
01    ST1:    uh::::::::: ST2? she: lived in NYC for four months,
02    TC:     nods
03    ST1:    [because of a/uh::: [schola?
              [gaze to ST2       [gaze to TC
04    TC:     .h a °sch↓olarship.°=
05    ST1:    =yes [scholarship.]
06    TC:          [ °isn't it.° ]        [a scholarship.
              [turns to pick up chalk [nods
07            >do you know how to spell that?< you know what that is?
```

In line 03, we see the student uttering an elongated sound of either *uh* or the indefinite article 'a.' This elongation might be the first indication that ST1 is having trouble producing the next word. Slightly before this elongation as she starts saying the word *because*, we also see her shift her gaze towards ST2—the source of this information that she is reporting on, which is potentially a second indication that she might need help with this next bit of her talk. Further, as ST1 starts with the word she seems to be having trouble with, she shifts her gaze to the teacher—the expert in the room, and she ends her yet-to-be completed word *schola* in a rising intonation. In other words, we have now received multiple clues to ST1's potential difficulty, none of which has escaped the teacher's discerning eyes. Indeed, her assistance is delivered in the next beat as she takes a short inbreath and provides *scholarship. isn't it* (lines 04 & 06) in a quiet voice and lowered pitch. Imagine the alternatives such as 'Can you repeat?' 'What are you trying to say?' or 'I don't get what you mean by *schola*.' With the delivery of *scholarship* at the exact moment when it is needed, the student is spared the ordeal of having to do all the work to get the help she needs. Help arrives without any unnecessary sweat on her part. That it is indeed the help she needs is evidenced in her repetition in line 05, and we then see the teacher proceed to offer further assistance to the entire class by turning this moment into a vocabulary lesson for the class (not shown).

Adjust as it goes

While the scenario above highlights the timing of contingent assistance, what makes contingent assistance *contingent* is also the fine-tuning of such assistance contingent upon, again, what is happening *now*—at this very second. We have one such example below from another adult ESL classroom, where the class is going over the vocabulary item 'ceremony.' See if you can spot the teacher's fine-tuning work in the way he provides assistance.

(3) ceremony [Waring, 2015, p. 73]
```
01    TC:      who can explain to me:: what a ↑ceremony is.
02    ST1:     a: special event?
03    TC:      [1.0
               [looks up at ST1
04             circular inducing hand gesture
05             to::::: what kind of special event.
06             (0.3)
07    ST2:     formal.
08    ST3:     like a [ ( )
09    TC:             [ a formal event? nods
```

ST1's explanation of 'ceremony' as *a special event* in line 02 is what would perhaps be considered partially correct, and the teacher seems to be treating it as such.

Now the question is, how does one provide the kind of assistance that would help the student develop the explanation further to get at the essence of 'ceremony.' Sometimes, providing assistance just means giving the gift of time or making room for someone to think. This is exactly what the teacher does in line 03 as he looks up at ST1 during the (1.0) second silence. This is done in lieu of offering the confirmation ST1 seems to be seeking. After all, ST1 is on the right track, and all she needs could be just a bit more time, and the (1.0) silence along with the gaze implicitly invites ST1 to continue.

What's important to notice here is that when ST1 does not continue, the teacher adds the gesture in line 04, thus upgrading his invitation. Then, when that gesture fails, he shifts to verbal means. In line 05, the teacher offers the infinitive *to* as way of assisting ST1 to expand her original explanation to specify the purpose of the *special event*. As can be seen, however, despite the elongated *to*, neither ST1 nor anyone else volunteers to complete the utterance, and the teacher switches tactic yet again, and this time, explicitly asks a *wh-* question. Student responses that continue to develop the explanation finally start to appear (lines 07 & 08).

What we can notice here is the teacher constantly acting upon the information he is gathering on the effectiveness of his own assistance and fine-tuning that assistance—millisecond by millisecond. This is different from repeating the same course of action again and again despite the failure of that action as we observed in the earlier portion of the 'endorphins' example (see Extract 1).

Assist anyway

If not providing contingent assistance is a matter of persisting regardless of what's happening, providing such assistance in part entails assisting regardless of whether what's happening fits with the teacher's agenda at the moment. The example below is taken from the same interaction around 'scholarship' shown earlier. By this point, the teacher has checked to see if everyone knows the word 'scholarship,' and ST3 has admitted that she doesn't know the word. As the extract begins, the teacher asks ST1 to explain the word to ST3. See if you can notice how the teacher provides assistance despite her focus on 'scholarship.' (Transcription note: ° = quiet voice.)

(4a) graduate and diploma [Boblett, 2020]
01   TC: explain that. to (.) °to ST3 what that is.°
02   ST1:   °uh:::::: scholarship (.) is like uh:° (0.8) when we:: (2.0)
03   do: >graduation?<

04	TC:	[(0.8)

```
04   TC:    [(0.8)
             [crosses arms, one hand to chin
05          okay, [after-        ] [after we gra]duate?
06   ST1:         [°after gradua- ] [after gra-°   ]
07          after we graduate?
```

We see that ST1 has a great deal of difficulty as she tries to explain scholarship in a soft voice. She begins her turn with an elongated *uh* that delays the explanation to come. This is followed by a micro-pause before she continues, and what ensues are further delays with elongations and pauses before she completes her explanation with *do graduation* in rising intonation and quickened pace with the word *graduation*. What she offers so far appears to be a far cry from 'scholarship,' and yet, watch what the teacher does.

You may notice some of the strategies we discussed earlier. Similar to what the teacher did in the prior extract, she gives the gift of time—the space to ponder, and in this case, to revise (line 04). Having provided that space, the teacher then goes on to produce an *okay* in a rising intonation before offering a recast beginning with *after* (line 05). At the same time, we see that that gift of time seems to be precisely what ST1 needed to arrive at the rephrasing of *do* into *after*. She then repeats the teacher's formulation *after we graduate* in line 07. Here we see another example of how contingent assistance is offered with such fine-tuned timing.

But more importantly for our purpose here is that the teacher provides assistance despite the fact that ST1's explanation doesn't seem relevant to the teacher's focus on 'scholarship' at the moment. Time is spent helping ST1 express what *she* needs to express. Assistance is offered contingent upon the student's need, not the teacher's agenda. This particular kind of contingent assistance continues as the teacher lets ST1 further her explanation of scholarship that begins with *graduation* and is now moving to *diploma*—an item she has trouble finding a word for.

(4b) graduate and diploma [Boblett, 2020]

```
08   ST1:   we: receive (0.8) [$s(h)ometh(h)ing hehhehheh$ .HHH
                              [turns to TE and gestures rectangle
09   TE:    ↑ah: (.) you receive a: like a [diploma
                                           [gestures rectangle
10          >or something I think it's a< li:ttle bit d↓ifferent than that?
```

In line 08, as ST1 searches for the word 'diploma,' she turns to the teacher and gestures 'rectangle' while at the same time using *something* in a laughing voice as a stand-in for the word she's looking for. Again, instead of dismissing ST1's continued explanation as irrelevant, the teacher provides the assistance that the latter needs (line 09) to complete that explanation despite its tangential relevance to the teacher's mini-lesson on 'scholarship.' And she only begins to launch a return to 'scholarship' after offering that contingent assistance (line 10).

In sum, we hope to have made it clear that attending to learner voice requires providing contingent assistance and that such assistance can be done through strategies such as **offer before the 'ask'**, **adjust accordingly**, and **assist anyway**. The 'contingent' requirement of providing contingent assistance demands that one be utterly other-attentive at the expense of all self-interests. Across the three strategies, the need to be present figures prominently. For us, this is one of the centerpieces of micro-reflection. You can't provide contingent assistance unless you are on the scene, and you can't be on the scene unless you listen—really listen—for signals that help is needed, that a different kind of help is needed, or that help should be dispatched despite your agenda at the moment. In addition to being present is the need to be ready—with a variety of ways of providing help that can be deftly tailored to that particular need in that particular moment. That means you cannot just have one way of offering help, and that persisting with the same tactic is what makes your help non-contingent. Sometimes, help comes in the form of silence—the space for the students to work out a problem, and sometimes it comes in the form of linguistic or gestural scaffolding. There is no predetermined recipe for what needs to be doled out for what situation, but having a variety of tools at the ready, or even just knowing the importance of trying different things to adapt to the moment, would be a great start.

Resources for Providing Contingent Assistance

(1) do syllable-by-syllable micro-listening and moment-by-moment micro-watching for clues of trouble (e.g., silence, gaze, gesture, posture, prosody)
(2) be ready to shift tactics as needed
(3) mind-read by staying other-focused (e.g., give the help needed, not force unnecessary guessing)
(4) use pauses, prosody, and gestures to give the gift of time
(5) provide clues to narrow the field of possibilities

Changing

So far, we have worked on noticing what types of teacher conduct are conducive to providing contingent assistance and what kinds of specific verbal and visible resources may be used to make that happen. While noticing serves as a prerequisite—and sets the stage—for changing, it does not automatically lead to change. A key component in our cycle of micro-reflection entails the work of instigating changes in one's conduct, and such work, as we argue, must be reflective in nature. As such, we offer a series of guided exercises to facilitate this reflective process of changing that moves from what to look for, to what to think about, and finally, to what to do.

What to look for

1. Based on your experiences as a student, a teacher, or an observer, what would you say might be three signs that the teacher is providing contingent assistance? More specifically, what would be some of the features of student conduct in those situations, and what would be some of the features of teacher conduct?

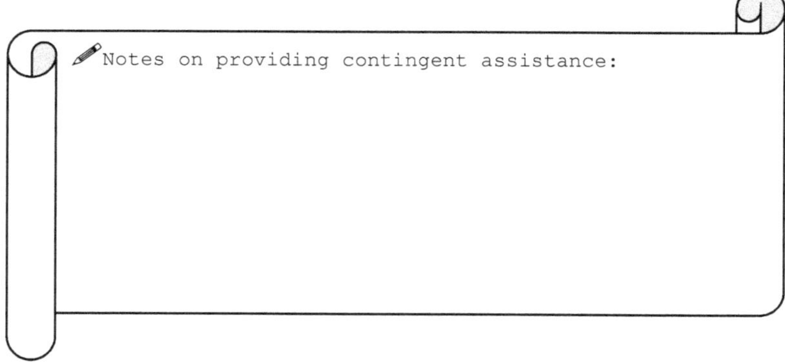

2. Take a look at the following extract. The class has been working on filling in the blanks with either the present perfect or present perfect progressive forms of particular verbs, and the specific item reads as: 'Since they started playing in 1926, more than 100 million people in over ninety different countries _____ (see) them.' What are some of the observable signs that the teacher is providing or not providing contingent assistance?

(5) have seen [Waring, 2016, p. 69]

```
01  ST1:    hav- have been looks tentatively up at TC
02          [seeing.    ]
03  TC:     [have been] seeing? walks back to BB
04          are you su::re?
05  SS:     (mumbling various things)
06  ST2:    °have see:n.°
07  TC:     let's write this down. writes item on board with blank
08          turns around okay, what's the correct answer.
09          (0.8)
10          since they started playing in 1926, more than 100 million
11          people in over ninety different countrie:::::s
12  ST3:    °haveh s[een.°]
13  TC:             [We  ]'re TA:LKING about SO:: FA:::R.
```

What to think about

1. In our noticing section above, we have given a flavor of what providing or not providing contingent assistance looks like. Take a moment to focus on the idea of providing contingent assistance and think of any other strategies (positive or negative) based on your experiences and/or observations as a teacher or a student. Be as specific as possible in your description of the strategy.

    (a) When is it done, how is it done, and what response(s) does it receive?
    (b) What words, gestures, intonation, and timing are used in its delivery?
    (c) What alternatives are available at time of its production?

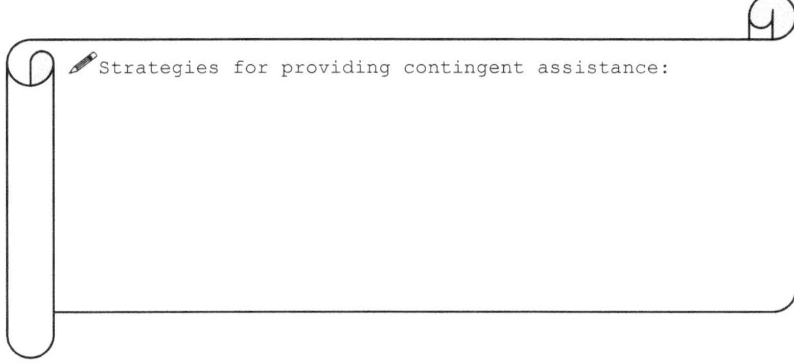

2. Consider an earlier extract (reproduced below). Recall that the class is working on the definition of 'endorphins' with a vocabulary-definition matching exercise based on a text that includes the word 'endorphin.' For each turn that the teacher takes, describe:
    (a) what alternatives there might be;
    (b) what she does precisely (e.g., X as opposed to Y);
    (c) what specific resources are used;
    (d) in what way the teacher's conduct might be considered providing or not providing contingent assistance;
    (e) how it is responded to;
    (f) what other choices there might be at this juncture to provide contingent assistance.

    (6) endorphins [Waring, 2015, p. 71]
    01 TE: okay, so from the sentence we can tell 'endorphins' mea:ns (0.8)
    02 ST1: chemicals that make us feel better.
    03 TC: okay.
    04   (0.8)
    05   and uh ST2 according to the <u>sen</u>tence 'endorphins' mea:ns (1.0)
    06 ST2: °it's the same word ( ) I can't explain ( )°
    07 TC: well- but according to the sentence,
    08   if we use the (.) kind of <u>c</u>ontext to help us. this sentence
    09   really tells us a<u>no</u>ther way to talk about the meaning right?
    10 ST?: °mhm°
    11   (3.5)
    12 TC: [<u>wh</u>at is that-]
    13 ST2: [(   )] I don't know! I can't explain in the
    14   sentence. when you know the word, it's difficult to explain.

3. In the following excerpt taken from an adult ESL classroom, the students have been working on vocabulary related to describing graphs (*increase, decrease*, etc.). To practice, they have drawn graphs of their experiences studying English. Here, one student is describing his graph. At each turn where the student does not speak, consider the following:
    (a) what the teacher could be doing at this particular juncture but is not;
    (b) what she does instead;
    (c) what interactional resources (verbal and visible) she uses to do what she does;

(d) in what way her choices might be demonstrating providing contingent assistance;

(e) how her conduct is received by the student;

(f) what other choices there might be at this juncture to provide contingent assistance.

(7) the effect [Fagan, 2015b, p. 84]

```
01  ST:    then (0.6) it (0.4) my level of studying (1.2) was increase
02         (1.4) increased rapidly.
03         [(4.0)
           [ST looks down; TC looks from class to ST
04         but in just for a month (3.2) it con- (1.0) it continued
05         (5.0) until twelve- twenty years old.
06         [(3.2)
           [ST looks down; TC looks around at class
07         I mean, (2.8) the (3.0) [effect?
                                   [starts looking at TC
08         [(1.2)
           [ST looks up completely; TC looks from class back to ST
09         [continued?
           [looks to TC
10  TC:    ↑ah. the effect,
11         [(0.4)
           [TC and ST nod
12  ST:    the [effect]
13  TC:       [the ef]fect?<
              [appears to contemplate
14         TC looks up as if contemplating
15         the e- yeah. I see what you mean. and I- I- I don't
16         know if I would say it quite like that.=
17         but- >good. good.< [continue.
                              [makes circular motion
```

What to do

1. Based on the skills you have developed so far, observe an actual lesson (with a video-camera if possible) with a specific focus on strategies for providing contingent assistance. Organize your notes using the following table.

Strategies for providing contingent assistance	
Strategies	Details
1. 2. 3.	(a) What could have been done differently at this particular moment in the interaction? (b) What is not being done, and why? (c) What exactly is being done, and how? (d) How is what is being done taken up by the participants in the data?
Strategies for not providing contingent assistance	
Strategies	Details
1. 2. 3.	(a) What could have been done differently at this particular moment in the interaction? (b) What is not being done, and why? (c) What exactly is being done, and how? (d) How is what is being done taken up by the participants in the data?

2. Repeat the same exercise above with a video-recording of your own teaching, and invite a colleague to either join the exercise or offer feedback on your own analysis.

3. With the observational materials you have gathered (video recordings preferably), identify moments where the teacher is providing contingent assistance and try to work backwards to figure out what has been done to lead to that moment.

4. Try out specific strategies for providing contingent assistance in your own class one at a time. Make note of each strategy's effect in terms of specific student conduct. Make adjustments accordingly as you repeat the exercise.

BUILDING ON STUDENT TALK

Along with providing contingent assistance, teachers can **attend to learner voices** by building on what students offer to the conversation. Building on student talk starts with noticing it in the moment, a skill which is directly related to the cycle of micro-reflection. Once we have honed our micro-noticing skills, we can move on to making reflective choices. Sometimes, it is enough to work with students to **develop** what they are saying. This is related to being open, which we discussed in Chapter 2, but is more precise. Rather than a general sense of openness, we are co-creating, along with a particular student, a specific stretch of talk that moves the interaction forward. Put differently, we are attending to learner voices by helping students use their voices. In other situations, we may choose to **embroider** on student talk. In these cases, we recycle student talk, and then add on to it, either using more technical, academic language, or actually adding intellectual complexity. Below, we look at examples of teachers as they **develop** and **embroider**. In order to clarify this skill, however, we start, with an example of not building on student's talk.

Noticing

Not building

Not building and not providing contingent assistance can look similar, since both seem to involve *not* noticing student talk. One difference, however, is that building can occur even when students have not displayed any trouble or confusion. It follows then, that we can find examples of teachers missing potential opportunities for building in moments when everything seems to be going as planned. In the example below, we see one brief moment of potential confusion, but we also see many students apparently participating in an activity with no trouble at all. The following extract takes place in a reading class in a community college, with young adult students. The teacher (TC) and students (ST1, ST2, etc.) are engaged in a vocabulary review where the teacher reads a brief definition, and students provide the matching vocabulary word. As the extract begins, the teacher reminds students to call out their answers (line 01), and then gives the first definition (line 02). The pattern that ensues is probably familiar to anyone who has spent much time in typical western classrooms.

(8) vocabulary review [Jacknick & Creider, 2018, p. 78]

```
01   TC:     alright? so down below you can just call these out,
02           to hypnotize or fascinate?
03   ST1:    desp[ise,  ]
04   ST2:        [mes ][merize.]
05   ST3:             [desp    ]ise.
06   ST1:             [>I mean<][mesmerize,]
07   ST4:                       [mesmerize,]
08   ST5:                       [mesmerize.]
09   TC:     $mesmerize$. a great or complete change?
10   SS:     metamorpho[sis.   ]
11   ST?:              [meto]morpho[sis. ]
12   TC:                          [cru]de or exaggerated?
13   SS:     [travesty.]
14   ST4:    [travesty ]?
15   ST2:    [travest  ]y.
16   TC:     done only as a routine? something you don't care about?
```

As we mentioned above, with just a few exceptions, students seem to have no trouble with this exercise. For instance, most students seem to respond to the definition *to hypnotize or fascinate* (line 02) with the correct response, which is *mesmerize* (lines 04 & 06–08). We do see first one student and then another call out an incorrect answer (lines 03 & 05), but at least one of them quickly corrects himself (line 06). In line 09, the teacher repeats the correct word and moves immediately on to the next definition, and several students quickly find the matching word (lines 10 & 11). We see this pattern repeat twice more in this extract (and, in fact, it continues for considerably longer in the video data). For the next two definitions (lines 12 & 16), the teacher doesn't explicitly acknowledge his students' correct answers, but simply moves on. One interesting point about this extract is that it includes something relatively rare in most adult classrooms, which is multiple students talking at the same time. Neither teacher nor students seem to mind the multiple instances of overlap, as students all shout out the same word at almost the same time. It is as if individual student voices are completely unimportant, as long as the 'correct' answer is spoken by someone. Thus, we see no attempt to draw students out, add complexity to the conversation, or respond in any, except the most cursory way, to student talk. Let's move on now to some examples of teachers actually responding skillfully to their students.

> **Strategies for building on student talk:** (1) develop; (2) embroider.

Develop

We start by looking at how teachers can build on student talk when they help students **develop** their turns. The following extract takes place in an adult ESL class. As the class begins, the teacher is asking her students about their weekends.

(9) weekend [Waring, 2016, p. 139]
```
01   TC:    oka:y, s↑o:, how was everyone's weekend.
02          (2.0)
03   ST:    (hh) it was goo (hh)od.
04   TC:    ST tell me about it.
05   ST:    I prepa:red- I bought ne:wspaper, I loo:ked through
06          it, I picked (0.2) [hh hh hh, an a:rticle,  ]
07   TC:                       [hh hh, a::ll weekend.]
08   ST:    no::. hh [hh]
09   TC:             [hh] hh.
```

10   ST: I sp(hh)ent it with my friends.
11   TC: go o:d, good good. did [you go anywhere special.]
12   ST: [(because) it was   ]
13   Valentine's Da:y, [a:nd   ] despi:te of the fa:ct that (.)=
14   TC: [a::::h.]
15   ST: my sweetie is in my (.) home cou:ntry?

After the teacher asks a general question (not directed to any specific student), we have a (2.0) second silence (lines 01 & 02). Notice that the teacher doesn't rush to fill this empty space, but just waits to see who might respond. The silence may serve to give students time to think, especially important for second language speakers. The next move we see from our teacher is more explicit. In line 04, after ST gives a brief answer (line 03), TC first says the student's name (transcribed as 'ST' here), and then says *tell me about it*. The use of the student's name is a way to personalize this request, and we can also notice that the teacher uses a first person pronoun (*me*), as opposed to saying 'tell **us** about it.' Thus, the teacher seems to imply that he is personally interested in what the student has to say. It's as if he were carving out the space for a one-on-one conversation in the middle of class. And, ST's response (lines 05 & 06) is considerably more extensive than her initial *good*. Our teacher doesn't stop here, however. In line 07, he responds to the content of what his student says, in a turn that is carefully timed to fit with the end of the student talk. This kind of timing, where one person starts talking just before someone else finishes, is typical of 'ordinary' (as opposed to classroom) conversations—it's something we all do without noticing it. We can also notice what the teacher does not do, namely correct his student. Instead, his talk seems designed to emphasize the fact that the student's response was focused on school-related activities—the teacher is subtly asking if ST spent *all weekend* studying. This seems to make space for the student to bring in more of her life outside of classroom, as she goes on to share not just that she spent the weekend with friends, but that her *sweetie* is far away (lines 10, 13, & 15). In line 11, the form of the teacher's response is slightly different. Notice that his first two responses were not phrased as questions, while this one is. In the context of the classroom, even the most innocuous questions can feel like tests (Creider, 2016). Thus, the teacher's opening *Tell me about it*, not phrased as a question, seems to serve as an invitation rather than as a quiz. By now, however, the conversational tone of the interaction is firmly established—and a specific, follow-up question only moves the interaction along. Similarly, the teacher's use of *good* in line 11 seems to be responding to the fact that the student saw friends over the weekend. In other words, this is not an assessment of the student's work in class, but rather a personal response to information the student chose to share with the teacher. Finally, we note the *ah* in line 14, which is yet another way of showing the student that her teacher is listening and interested. Thus, this interaction is full of subtle signals of interest on the part of the teacher, as well as carefully constructed responses that help ST **develop** an initially brief answer into something more extensive.

Embroider

We use the term **embroider** to describe moments when we see teachers add complexity to the students' talk, just as one might add colorful stitches to a sewing project. This requires both careful attention to student talk *and* a deep understanding of the subject matter at hand. By their very nature, these moments are unplanned, since teachers do not know ahead of time what a student might say or do. Thus, in order to build on student voices via embroidery, teachers must reflectively keep track of their own pedagogical goals, as well as student needs, and student language in the moment. To explore this skill, let's look at the following extract, where a tutor is working on math with a four-year-old emergent-bilingual French/English speaker. Tutor (TR) and tutee (TT) are sitting on the floor doing math games with poker chips, and there is a pile of different kinds of chips on the floor in front of them.

(10a) pretty old [Creider, 2013, p. 13]
```
01    TR:     well, (.) [I thoug]ht first [we-]
02    TT:            [(this)  ]        [the ]se look pretty old.
03    TR:     they are pretty old yes.
```

As this excerpt starts, the tutor is making a suggestion. She is probably going to describe the first step of an activity (*I thought first we...*). However, her tutee is more interested in the objects in front of her, and she announces that the chips *look pretty old*. This brings us to an interesting choice point (Hepburn et al., 2014, p. 248). The tutor could ignore the interruption and keep speaking, or even ask her tutee to stop talking and just listen. We can imagine several ways for a tutor to accomplish this kind of action, including holding up a finger in a 'wait' gesture, or saying something like 'just a minute.' Instead, the tutor briefly acknowledges her tutee's words in line 03. Here, again, we can imagine her simply acknowledging, and then going back to her plan. Let's see what she actually does.

(10b) pretty old [Creider, 2013, p. 13]

04		(0.2)
05	**TR:**	**uh I'll show you let's see (I know the really old)**
06	TT:	huhhuh
07	**TR:**	**here this is the old kind the dark colored ones are the old kind**
08		[(1.0)
		[*TR looking through chips*
09	**TR:**	**[oh this is one of the old ones see how it's kind of worn out looking**
		[*picking up a chip, turning it in her hand, holding it towards TT*
10		*hands chip to TT* **and softer?**
11	TT:	*nods slightly*
12	TR:	Feel it with your fingers.
13	TT:	[\$aha it's] softee\$
		[*touching chip*
14	TR:	[>(if you can feel how it's soft)<]

After a brief pause, the tutor announces that she's going to show the tutee something, and then starts sorting through the chips to find the *old kind* (line 07). At first glance, this seems like she's just following along with the child's interest. And, indeed, the tutor has put her agenda on hold to follow her tutee's interest in old chips. But our tutor is doing more here. If we look closely at her language, she also **embroiders** on her tutee's initial contribution, upgrading a simple description of a few chips into an approach to sorting the chips. (Sorting is a math readiness activity, commonly taught to children of this age.) The tutor does this by shifting from talking about specific chips to discussing *the old kind* (line 07), and then moving on to talking about *the old ones* (line 09). Both phrases suggest that 'old chips' are a class or group which can be described and discussed. Our tutor also provides concrete descriptions of 'old' chips, saying that they are *dark colored* (line 07), *worn out looking*, and *softer* (lines 09 & 10). In a sense, the tutor is teaching her tutee how to pay attention to the chips as members of classes that can be given general descriptions, rather than as individual objects.

In our next example, we will see the same tutor (TR), working this time with a five-year-old emergent bilingual Spanish-English speaker (TT). TR and TT and sitting together on the ground, with a pile of multicolored dice in front of them. This extract is interesting in that what gets embroidered on is not simply specific words, but the tutee's gesture plus a simple expression of interest. Let's look at how our tutor responds when the tutee picks up a die (line 02), an action which could have been brushed off or ignored.

(11) this one [Creider data]
01   **TR:**   **can we fin[d all the]**
02   TT: [oh I did]n't saw *picking up a die* this one.
03   **TR:**   **oh** *taking die from TT* **<u>th</u>at one's neat**
04   **[look it's got a <u>blue: pa:rt</u>,**
             [*pointing at dots on die*
05   **(0.2) and a <u>gree:n pa:rt</u>, (.)**
06   **[it's green like your shirt**
             [*pointing at TT's shirt*
07   *TT looks down at shirt* (0.2)
08   TT: yeah
09   **TR:**   **and there's <u>y</u>ellow:, (0.4) and there's <u>ora</u>:nge, (0.2)**
10   *TR holds die to shirt sleeve while TT looks at shirt sleeve*
11   **°I think it's the same orange as your shirt°**
12   *TT moves head and exhales loudly* (0.6)
13   TT: [<and what's thi:s?>
             [*picking up blue die*

In line 01, TR starts to make a suggestion. She is interrupted by her tutee, who picks up a die and announces that he hadn't seen it before (line 02). Rather than asking TT to wait, or to listen, TR takes the die and begins to talk about it (line 03). She starts to point to the different colors on the die, naming each color and comparing them to TT's clothing (lines 04–06, 09, & 11). For a young emergent bilingual student, this builds the skill of naming colors in English. In addition, comparing the traits of objects (in this case die and clothing) is an important mathematical concept for students of this age. Thus, our tutor takes her student's brief gesture and expression of interest, and **embroiders** on it, adding both linguistic information (colors), and the idea that objects can be compared (mathematical complexity).

Let's take a closer look at the resources for **embroidering** we've discussed thus far. Just as we discussed in the section on providing contingent assistance, our own ability to listen and watch closely are perhaps the most important resource for building. However, rather than noticing moments of trouble, the goal is to find what we call 'buildable materials.' Materials, in this case, are not bricks and mortar, but rather student conduct. As we have described above, teachers can build on students' words, and even their gestures (e.g., picking up a die). Once we learn to catch these moments, they become resources. If we want to help a student move the conversation forward, we can make sure that they know that we are actually interested in what they are saying, for instance, by using their names. We can also pause for a moment to allow students to think, or even ask follow-up questions. Note that this kind of question is not designed to find out what a student knows, but is rather a genuine request for information. When we **develop** student turns, we are putting the student in the role of expert, and simply helping them to showcase what they have to say. We can also actually recycle student language, and then add on technical or academic terms. Here, we are essentially 'translating' what a student says from everyday language to more formal, academic language. This can be especially helpful for young language learners who are trying to simultaneously learn English and learn pedagogical content. Finally, we can move yet one step further and actually bring new ideas into the conversation, as we use displays of interest on the part of a student to add pedagogical complexity to the interaction.

Resources for Building

(1) do syllable-by-syllable micro-listening and moment-to-moment micro-watching to identify buildable materials
(2) engage with students on a one-on-one level to draw them out (e.g., use students' names, look directly towards them)
(3) use pauses or follow-up questions to make space for students to continue speaking
(4) recycle student language
(5) add technical or academic language onto student language (e.g., *type*)
(6) add pedagogical complexity to student interests (e.g., comparing traits of die and clothing)

Changing

Now that we have started to notice how teachers can build on student contributions, it is time to reflect on this strategy in your own teaching. As ever, we suggest that the first step in reflecting on real-life teaching is knowing what to look for in both our students' and our own actions.

What to look for

1. Based on your experiences as a student and as a teacher, when would building be an appropriate response to a student contribution?
2. Based on your experiences as a student and as a teacher, what might be three signs that a teacher is building? What would be some of the features of student conduct in those situations, and what would be some of the features of teacher conduct?

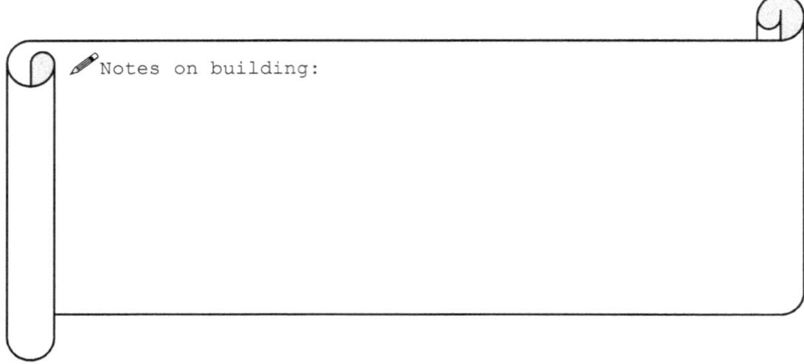

3. Consider the following excerpt, where a student is reporting on a graph of his studying habits. For each line in bold type below, think about the following:

(a) what alternatives there might be;

(b) what the teacher does precisely;

(c) what specific resources are used;

(d) in what way the teacher's conduct might be building;

(e) how it is responded to;

(f) what other choices there might be at this juncture to build.

(12) the effect [Fagan, 2015b, p. 84]

01 ST: then (0.6) it (0.4) my level of studying
02   (1.2) was increase (1.4) increased rapidly.
03   [(4.0)
                 [*ST looks down; TC looks from class to ST*
04   but in just for a month (3.2) it con- (1.0) it continued
05   (5.0) until twelve-twenty years old.
06   [(3.2)
                 [*ST looks down; TC looks around at class*
07   I mean, (2.8) the (3.0) [effect?
                                      [*starts looking at TC*
08   [(1.2)
                 [*ST looks up completely; TC looks from class back to ST*
09   [continued?
             [*looks to TC*

10	TC:	↑ah. the effect,
11		[(0.4)
		[*TC and ST nod*
12	ST:	the [effect]
13	TC:	[*the* ef]fect?<
		[*appears to contemplate*
14		[(1.0)
		[*TC looks up as if contemplating*
15		the e- [yeah. i see what you mean. and i- i- i don't
		[*looks at ST*
16		know if I would say it quite like that.=
17		but- >good. good.< [continue.
		[*makes circular motion*
18		[(0.4)
		[*TC looks at ST; ST looks at paper*
19	TC:	°that's good.°
20	ST:	[since twenty years old-
21	TC:	[*points to ST's chart as a reminder*
22	ST:	(0.4) twenty-seven=
23	TC:	[years old
24	ST:	[*nods*
25	TC:	=mhm?
26	ST:	<↑u:h, (1.2) it (2.0) it decreased (0.2) gradually.

What to think about

1. In our noticing section above, we have drawn attention to some strategies for building, including **developing** and **embroidering**. The lists are most definitely not exhaustive. Take a moment to focus on the idea of building on student contributions and think of any other strategies (positive or negative) based on your experiences and/or observations as a teacher or a student. Be as specific as possible in your description of the strategy.

   (a) When is it done (e.g., initiating or responsive position), how is it done, and what response(s) does it receive?

   (b) What words, gestures, intonation, and timing are used in its delivery?

   (c) What alternatives are available at the time of its production?

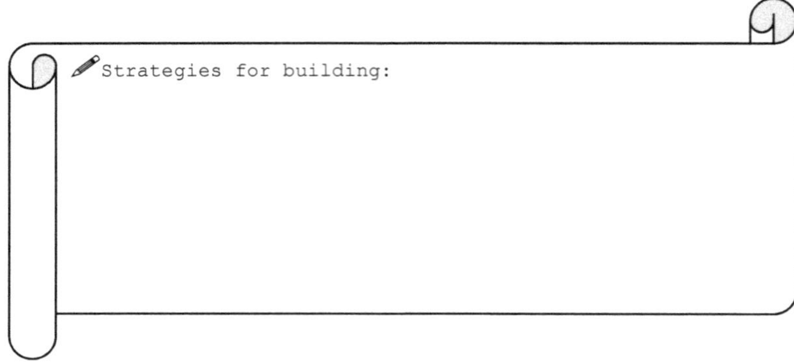

2. Consider the following extract that demonstrates how **embroidering** can be done. This is a math tutoring lesson with a five-year old. For each turn that the tutor (TR) takes, describe:
    (a)   what alternatives there might be;
    (b)   what she does precisely (e.g., X as opposed to Y);
    (c)   what specific resources are used;
    (d)   in what way the tutor's conduct might be considered 'building';
    (e)   how it is responded to;
    (f)   what other choices there might be at this juncture to do 'building.'

    (13) green ones [Creider, 2013, p. 11]
    01   TR: OK (.) Two more blue ones
    02   [and then
    03   TT: [(uninte[lligible)
                        [*picks up a green die*
    04   (0.6)
    05   TR: you wanna find the green ones let's find the
    06   green ones
    07   TT: (let's find)
    08   TR: you see more- [gr]
    09   TT: [a] gre[en]
    10   TR: [a g]ree:n o:ne, put the
    11   green ones [right he:re
                        [*points to mat*
    12   TT: *starts a pile of green dice*
    13   TR: so many gree:n o::nes::

14	TT:	green one
15	TR:	a <u>gree:n o:ne</u>
16	TT:	a <u>gree:n o:ne</u>
17	TR:	another gree:n o:ne:

What to do

1. Based on the skills you have developed so far, observe an actual lesson (with a video-camera if possible) with a specific focus on strategies for (not) building. Organize your notes using the following table.

Strategies for building	
Strategies	Details
1. 2. 3.	(a) What could have been done differently at this particular moment in the interaction? (b) What is not being done, and why? (c) What exactly is being done, and how? (d) How is what is being done taken up by the participants in the data?
Strategies for not building	
Strategies	Details
1. 2. 3.	(a) What could have been done differently at this particular moment in the interaction? (b) What is not being done, and why? (c) What exactly is being done, and how? (d) How is what is being done taken up by the participants in the data?

5. Repeat the same exercise above with a video-recording of your own teaching, and invite a colleague to either join the exercise or offer feedback on your own analysis.

6. With the observational materials you have gathered (video recordings preferably), identify moments where students seem to understand instructions or content, and try to work backwards to figure out what has been done to lead to that moment.

Chapter 4

Balance Competing Demands

It is rare for teachers to have the luxury of focusing on one task, or one individual. Most of our time in the classroom is marked by a careful balancing of competing demands. Indeed, one of the reasons we find reflection to be such an important teaching skill is that it can help us skillfully handle the many, and sometimes conflicting, goals inherent in our work. We can begin by asking what we mean by 'balance.' Sometimes, it is a question of making conscious choices about our priorities. For instance, we may have noticed that some students tend to remain silent during whole class discussions. After reflecting on this tendency, we might choose to prioritize bringing out these students' voices, even at the cost of not opening the floor to other more talkative students. Here, balance is something that occurs not in a single moment, but over the course of a whole class, or even a whole semester. At other times, we can take advantage of what Waring (2016) calls the 'multivocalic' quality of teacher talk. As Waring writes, everything we say or do in the classroom 'can do more than one thing, bringing into relief a range of concerns inhabiting the classroom: order, equity, learning, participation, progressivity, and inclusiveness, namely, the multiple and potentially competing demands that teachers manage on a moment-by-moment basis' (p. 95). Thus, if we can notice and reflect on this quality, we can take advantage of it—creating balance moment-by-moment, as we simultaneously attend to multiple demands. This sounds complex—and, in some ways it is! It requires careful attention to both our students and ourselves. But it can also be as simple as holding out our hand towards one student as we listen to another, or infusing warmth into our voice as we respond to a student's description of her weekend.

In one sense, the primary balancing act required of teachers (and students) in the classroom has to do with the reality that along with being teachers and students, we are also human beings (also see Farrell, 2019). This sounds obvious, but, in fact, it can make classroom interactions complicated. For instance, students may need to balance the wish to learn and understand new material with the wish to sound and act competent. Similarly, a teacher may want to listen to one student's story about their weekend but may simultaneously be thinking about the needs of the rest of the students in the classroom. Or, what about the teacher in an adult language class who needs to ask a pair of students not to talk to each other during a whole-class activity? As a teacher, she is thinking about the fact that those students are potentially missing out on important information, and that they may be distracting the other students. At the same time, as an adult speaking to other adults, she wants to preserve their sense of independence, to be polite, and to avoid conflict. Most teachers can come up with many other, similar examples. In this chapter, then, we start by noticing such moments, with the understanding that when we look closely at the competing demands with which we are faced, we can begin to reflect on how to balance them. We then move on to examining the tools used by skillful teachers to handle two kinds of competing demands: those related to multiple agendas, and those related to participation.

BALANCING AGENDAS

Most of us would agree that students learn best when they have a sense of independence in the classroom, and when they feel connected to the topics at hand. It makes sense that attending to student interests and student agency is an important part of the work of being a teacher. Indeed, in our experience, most teachers instinctively want to preserve their students' autonomy and to follow student interests. At the same time, many of the tasks that are considered crucial for teachers seem to be in direct conflict with these goals. From taking attendance, to following a lesson plan, or making sure that students take turns when they speak in class (Creider, 2016; Waring, 2014), a teacher's work can feel like an exercise in being in charge and sticking to the plan. One way to think about this dilemma is to see it as a question of balancing competing agendas. On one side is the agenda of encouraging student agency and paying attention to students' own interests. On the other side is the agenda related to the institutional job of running a classroom. In this section, we look at tools that teachers can use as they attend to *both* of these aspects of their work.

Noticing

> **Strategies for balancing agendas:** (1) share the work; (2) redirect humorously; (3) weave.

As we discuss above, most instances of balancing competing agendas have to do with acting as a teacher, with all of the power and control that the role entails, versus acting as a person in a non-institutional role, a person who hopes to build connection and share power. As we explore this dilemma, we look at several different types of scenarios. We start this section with an example of how teachers may balance conflicting agendas to pre-empt a conflict with a student.

Share the work

In our own experience, giving instructions is one moment when the question of how to balance agendas can feel particularly fraught. After all, giving instructions does involve telling students what to do—and few people, no matter what their age, relish taking orders from someone else. However, if we avoid explicitly telling students what we want them to do, there is almost no way to organize any kind of classroom work. This is where carefully reflecting on our language choices can be useful. In the following excerpt, the tutor (TR) is working on math skills with a six-year-old emergent bilingual Spanish English tutee (TT). They are seated on the floor, and are about to do an activity using poker chips to make different combinations of numbers that equal ten (5+5, 4+6, etc.). As we will see, the first step of the activity is to make a horizontal row of ten chips.

(1) in a row [Creider, 2012, p. 65]

01	TR:	let's put 'em a::ll: in a row.
02		[one, [two, three, four, five, six, seven, eight,]
		[*moves chip to row with each number*
03	TT:	[two, three, four, five, six, seven, eight,]
04		[nine, ten.
		[*moves a chip to row with each number*
05	TR:	[nine, ten. so that's ten so,

Let's think about all the ways a teacher could introduce the idea of making a row of ten poker chips. The most obvious is probably to simply tell the student to do it, as in 'Make a row of 10 chips.' Maybe, in order to be polite, the teacher might add 'please.' Or, perhaps equally common, this request could be phrased as a question:

'Can you make a row of 10 chips?' Most students would know perfectly well that this is actually a command, disguised as a question. However, in this case, our tutor does something different. She uses the phrase *let's*, which implies that the work of making the row is something for which she and her tutee are equally responsible. Thus, instead of a situation where one person (the tutor or teacher) gives the orders, and the other person (the student or tutee) does the work, TR has used one tiny phrase to create an atmosphere of cooperation and shared responsibility while still making sure that her planned activity moves forward. Her next move is even more interesting. She starts to make the row of chips herself (line 02). In many cases, of course, it's important for students themselves to engage with the objects and activities that make up a lesson plan. In this moment, however, TR makes a different choice. She uses her actions to make it clear that she is going to **share the work** of this activity. And, interestingly, the tutee joins in of her own accord, first naming the numbers of each chip with her tutor (line 03), and then taking over to move the final two chips on her own (line 04).

Redirect humorously

In the above scenario, potential resistance is pre-empted as the teacher **shares the work** of both building and following the instruction. In other words, she takes into account the tutee's agenda of autonomy as she gives directions. Sometimes, however, this kind of pre-emptive balancing isn't possible, and we find ourselves in a situation where students act in ways that conflict with our need to move forward with a lesson. Using humor is one way to balance our need to respond to difficult student behavior with the simultaneous need to avoid conflict with our students. In the following example, which is from an adult ESL class, a teacher is taking attendance while also checking in with students about how they are doing, what they did over the weekend, etc. However, as the excerpt starts, two students (ST1 and ST2) are apparently chatting with each other, rather than paying attention to the teacher or to other students.

(2) gossiping [Waring, Reddington, & Tadic, 2016, p. 32]
```
01    TC:      so:, ↑very nice [°(    ) good.°
                                [looks down
02             .hhhh [ST1
                     [looks up at ST1
03    ST1:     [( )
               [raises hand
04    TC:      so tell me what are you and ST2 gossiping
```

05		°**about over there,**° *checks in book*
06	ST1:	uhhhehehhh about- the: [(.) our ↑d]ogs?
07	ST2:	[kids.]
08	SS:	[hehheheheheh]
09	TC:	[about your [dogs?]
10	ST1:	[yes,]
11		ask he:r if she works (.) u:h ( )
12	TC:	mhm?
13	ST1:	↑yes she do(hhh)es hehehheh
14	TC:	and how are your kids doing.

The teacher's *so, very nice* (line 01) refers to something said by a previous student. We then see him look down (line 02), perhaps at a list of student names. Next, he calls ST1's name, and—in response—the student looks up and raises her hand. It is here, in line 04, that things get interesting. Note that the teacher is already engaged in what we might call the 'institutional task' of taking attendance. For many teachers, keeping track of which students are in class is required by administration. At the very least, it is a job that emphasizes the teacher's role as someone who is in charge in the classroom. At the same time, if we think about the students' point of view, attendance taking is not really a time when they can expect to learn new material—so it might make sense to use this section of class to chat with friends. The teacher, however, does not seem to be comfortable with this choice on the part of ST1 and ST2. And, given that this is a language class, we can imagine a teacher wanting to use this time to practice more social conversations in the target language. Indeed, one of the complex aspects of the language classroom is that even conversations that seem off topic can be opportunities for language learning. It could be, then, that the teacher wants his students to practice their listening skills at this moment. That said, he doesn't actually tell ST1 and ST2 to stop talking. Instead, he explicitly notices their behavior, using the joking formulation of *gossiping* (line 04). He also asks them about the topic of their conversation, thus **redirecting** their private conversation into a way to practice English, and into a conversation that the whole class can hear.

Weave

While dealing with potentially unwanted behaviors can call for a light touch, responding to unexpected topics or displays of interest may be even more tricky, especially if what the student is interested in doesn't fit with our pedagogical goals. How can a teacher simultaneously follow a student's lead and also follow their own lesson plan? In these cases, one option is for the teacher to show they are at least listening respectfully to their students, by **weaving** student language into their own talk (Creider, 2020). In the excerpt that follows, an experienced tutor does just that. Our tutor (TR) is working on a math lesson with a young tutee (TT). As the excerpt starts, there seems to be a clear conflict about what to do with a pile of poker chips which the tutor is using to teach sorting skills to her tutee.

(3a) red ones [Creider, 2013, p. 5]
```
01    TR:      make a pi- [start a pile of red
                          [patting the floor
02             ones. °here, let's make a pile of red ones.°
03             (.)
04             there's red ones,
```

TR starts by asking TT to make a pile of red chips. However, the tutee doesn't seem interested in going along with plan. Note the tiny bit of silence in line 03—a moment when we might have expected TT to start with her pile. The tutor responds to this silence by taking yet another tack. This time, she simply announces that there are red chips, perhaps hoping that TT will take over from here and start gathering the red ones. Let's see what the tutee does.

(3b) red ones [Creider, 2013, p. 5]
```
05    TT:      a:nd the same size.
06    TR:      yeah those are all the same size.
07    TT:      makes a pile of chips
08    TR:      there's a lot of red ones.
09    TT:      collecting red chips in her hand (   ) we
10             could collect all of these.
11             still collecting red chips
12    TR:      [(we could/ya gonna collect)]
13    TT:      [we could collect            ] them into different si-
14             into the same sizes.
```

In line 05, rather than starting to find red chips, TT makes a noticing statement of her own. Her focus, however, is on the size of the chips, rather than their color. TR now has a dilemma. She could give a direct order: 'TT, find all the red chips.' Or, she could abandon her project of sorting by color, and sort by size. Instead, she chooses a middle ground. (In an interview after this tutoring session, the tutor remarked that there simply weren't enough chips of different sizes to complete the sorting activity she had in mind, so she made the choice to stay with her original plan of sorting by color.) In line 06, the tutor responds to and echoes the tutee's turn, repeating the phrase *the same size*. In line 07, TT continues her initiation non-verbally, making a pile of chips based presumably on size (or at least not based on color). TR seems to ignore what TT is actually doing, and continues to talk about chip color, saying *there's a lot of red ones* (line 08). (By not commenting on TT's actions, the tutor may be avoiding treating the action as resistance.) Then, in line 09, TT seems to start to follow TR's suggestion as she gathers red chips into her hand. However, she then goes on to say: *we could collect them into different si- into the same sizes* (lines 13 & 14). TT, then, is still intent on her original proposal, first stated in line 05. How can TR handle this insistence?

(3c) red ones [Creider, 2013, p. 5]

15	**TR:**	**we could >collect them into the same sizes< but let's**
16		**collect them- we could collect them by <u>colors</u> too.**
17		**we could make piles of <u>each</u> color.**
18	TT:	*collecting a pile of different colored chips* I- I like to make
19		my own little pile.
20	**TR:**	**make your <u>pi:le</u>, (0.2) take your pile and make- make-**
21		**see how (.) high a pile you can make of red ones OK.**
(lines omitted)		
22	TR:	so you're making a pile of red ones. I think I'll make
23		a pile of yellow ones.

In line 15, TR starts by echoing exactly what TT has said, copying the previous turn almost word for word. She then says *but let's collect them- we could collect them by colors too*. In other words, the tutor combines the tutee's words with her own, designing a turn that **weaves** together tutor and tutee language. In lines 18 & 19, the tutee makes what seems like a bid for independence, gathering chips of all different colors and saying *I like to make my own little pile*. (Note: *little* may be a way to soften what is essentially a disagreement with her tutor and with the adult.) TR responds by again echoing TT's language: *make your pile* (line 20), and then returns to the idea of sorting by color. Thus, while the tutor does not follow the tutee's idea of sorting by size, she does acknowledge a bid for agency, telling her tutee to make her own pile, before returning to the task at hand. The two go on to sort the chips based on color.

Weaving, then, like so many of the practices we describe here, starts with reflective noticing. The first step is for the teacher to realize that a student is showing a divergent interest. She can then **weave** the interest into the lesson, for instance recycling her student's language, **weaving** the student's words into her own. Just as when teachers **share the work** or **redirect humorously**, this strategy asks teachers to pay attention to multiple needs at once, and to be ready to shift their linguistic choices in the moment.

The three strategies in this section all show how teachers can attend to their students' needs without putting other work on hold. In each case, the first step seems to be simply noticing that there is something to attend to. Beginning teachers are often so focused on tasks such as giving instructions that they don't pay attention to how their verbal and non-verbal choices may affect students in the moment. Once a teacher is aware of the need to balance competing agendas, it is through apparently minor shifts in word choice and tone that she can achieve this complex work. For instance, the tone of voice with which a teacher asks students what they are 'gossiping' about might make all the difference between whether the students feel that the teacher is joking or teasing. Similarly, by repeating the exact words a student uses, rather than a paraphrase, a teacher can signal that she is truly listening to her students, even if she is unable to follow their suggestions. Let's look at some of the resources we've seen teachers use in this section:

> **Resources for Balancing Agendas**
>
> (1) use *let's* and *we* to show shared responsibility
> (2) complete activities along with students
> (3) name disruptive activities with humor (e.g., gossip)
> (5) recycle student language word-for-word in your talk

Changing

So far, we have engaged the reader to notice what types of teacher conduct are conducive to balancing agendas and what kinds of specific verbal and visible resources may be used to carry out the relevant conduct. While noticing serves as a prerequisite, and sets the stage for changing, it does not automatically lead to change. A key component in our cycle of micro-reflection entails the work of instigating changes in one's conduct, and such work, as we argue, must be reflective in nature. As such, we offer a series of guided exercises to facilitate this intrinsically reflective process of changing that moves from what to look for, to what to think about, and finally, to what to do.

What to look for

1. Based on your experiences as a student, a teacher, or an observer, what would you say might be some signs that a teacher should attend to in balancing agendas? What would be some of the features of the student conduct in those situations, and what would be some of the features of the teacher conduct?

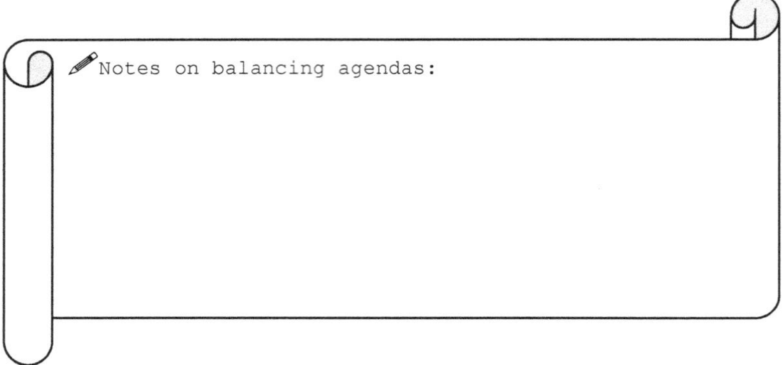

2. Consider the following extract from a tutoring session where a tutor (TR) is working on language and mathematics with a five-year old tutee (TT). What does the teacher do (or not do) to balance agendas?

(4) this is a car [Creider, 2013, p. 8]
01   TR: °you're making it all threes in a row°
02   (.)
03   [three dots, three dots.
            [*pointing at dice in a line*
04   TT: all that this is a car.
05   TR: are those cars.
06   TT: *nods*
07   TR: yeah but let's see (.) let's count the colors of the cars.
08   (.)
09   TR: give me your finger.
10   TT: *puts out finger*
11   TR: [pink car, green car,
            [*guides TT's finger across dice*
12   red car, red car, blue car, black car, red car, <u>with white dots,</u>
13   red car with <u>black</u> do:ts.

14 TT: *places a red die in line*
15 TR: another red car.

What to think about

1. In our noticing section above, we have drawn attention to a variety of strategies teachers may use to balance conflicting agendas. In particular, we discussed the dilemma of simultaneously doing the work of being a teacher (taking attendance, following a lesson plan, etc.) *and* focusing on student needs, or encouraging student independence. With a focus on the idea of balancing agendas, think of any other strategies for balancing (positive or negative), based on your experiences and/or observations as a teacher or a student. Be as specific as possible in your description of the strategy.
    (a) When is it done (e.g., initiating or responsive position), how is it done, and what response(s) does it receive?
    (b) What words, gestures, intonation, and timing are used in its delivery?
    (c) What alternatives are available at the time of its production?

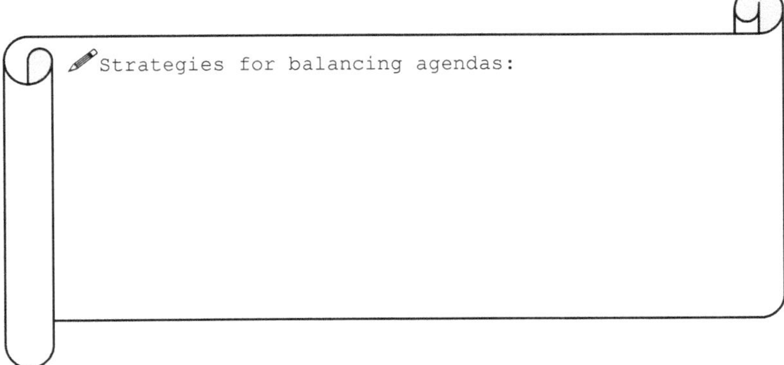

2. Consider the following extract from an adult ESL class. The students have been sharing how they spent Halloween weekend, when the teacher notices that three students—ST1, ST2, and ST3—are talking to each other, rather than joining in the whole-class activity. For each of the bolded turns below, note:
    (a) what the teacher could be doing at this particular juncture but is not;
    (b) what she does instead;

(c)   what interactional resources (verbal and visible) she uses to do what
      she does;
(d)   in what way her choices might be demonstrating balancing agendas;
(e)   how her conduct is received by the student;
(f)   what other choices there might be at this juncture to do balancing.

(5)   wanna share [Waring, Reddington, & Tadic, 2016, p. 35]

01	**TR:**	[okay, very [**good. .hh** *mock scowls*
		[*gaze at ST4, smiles and nods* [*gaze at ST1, ST2, and ST3*
02		$↑what are you three <doing.> exactly.$
03	SS:	*gaze at ST1, ST2, and ST3*
04		hhhhh
05	**TR:**	[**what are you looking** $at.$ *shakes head, smiles*
		[*gaze at ST1, ST2, and ST3*
06		(2.0) *ST1, ST2, and ST3 still looking at phone and talking*
07		*ST1, ST2, and ST3 look up*
08	**TR:**	[hhhh]
09	SS:	[hhhh]
10	**TR:**	$so what's going o:n. wanna sha:re?$
11	ST1:	(what?)
12	**TR:**	[<$what are you↑talking about.$>
		[*shakes head*
13	ST1:	( )
14	ST2:	hh ( )
15	ST1	(telling) that I was in a wedding this
16		↑weekend, so I was (showing pictures.)
17	**TR:**	**was it a Hallowee:n <u>the:</u>med wedding?** *smiles*
18	ST1:	no.
19	**TR:**	[n(h)o(h).] (.) *smiles* <u>th</u>at
		[*shakes head*
20		**would've been fun.=okay, ↑whose <u>wedding</u> was it.**
21	ST1:	my <u>cou</u>sin's wedding.
22	**TR:**	**your ↑cousin's wedding. (.)** *tilts head-* **>did you**
23		**have fun?<**
24	ST1:	$#of course.#$
25	**TR:**	[o: (h):h(h)o(h)h(h)o.
		[*smiles*
26	ST1:	it was (.) a<u>maz</u>ing.

27 TR: $o:::kay,$ <u>wh</u>ere was it.

28 ST1: m:::: Jersey?

29 TR: New Jersey? (.) *nods-* tsk okay.

30   (0.2)

31 ST1: I saw my family.

32 **TR: [aww, all your family. that's**
           **[*tilts head*

33   **pretty cool. did you da:nce?** *smiles*

34 ST1: y(h)eah.

35 SS: hhhhh

36 **TR: hhh (was-) what kind of music was it.**

37 ST1: it was more American?

38 TR: mhm,

39 ST1: bu::t, people li- liked the music though, (lines omitted)

40 **TR: °well: (.) make an impression I guess.° ST2 did**

41   **you go somewhere for Halloween?**

What to do

1. Based on the skills you have developed so far, observe an actual lesson (with a video-camera if possible) with a specific focus on strategies for balancing agendas. Organize your notes using the following table.

Strategies for balancing agendas	
Strategies	Details
1.	(a) What could have been done differently at this particular moment
2.	in the interaction?
3.	(b) What is not being done, and why?
	(c) What exactly is being done, and how?
	(d) How is what is being done taken up by the participants in the data?

Strategies for not balancing agendas	
Strategies	Details
1.	(a) What could have been done differently at this particular moment
2.	in the interaction?
3.	(b) What is not being done, and why?
	(c) What exactly is being done, and how?
	(d) How is what is being done taken up by the participants in the data?

2. Repeat the same exercise above with a video-recording of your own teaching, and invite a colleague to either join the exercise or offer feedback on your own analysis.
3. With the observational materials you have gathered (video recordings preferably), identify moments where the teacher is balancing agendas and try to work backwards to figure out what has been done to lead to that moment.
4. Try out specific strategies for balancing agendas in your own class one at a time. Make note of their effect in terms of specific student conduct. Make adjustments accordingly as you repeat the exercise.

BALANCING PARTICIPATION

Participation is a staple concern among practicing teachers. How do we avoid having the same few students dominate the classroom floor, how do we get the silent students to talk, and how do we distribute our attention between 'this student' and 'the other students'? These are among some of the most commonly raised questions for teachers-in-training. Balancing participation speaks to the difficulties of achieving even participation within the space and time constraints of a given classroom. These difficulties are elegantly articulated in what Reddington (2018) calls the 'participation paradox,' that is, 'the necessity of engaging in and disengaging from interactions with individual students to create opportunities for both extended and even participation' (p. 1). Although a clear case of un-balanced participation is where the teacher dominates the classroom floor with little student participation—also a symptom of an uninviting environment (see Chapter 2), our interest in this chapter concerns a lack of balance when students do participate—when the same few students speak all the time, or when the individual is attended to at the expense of the group (or vice versa). Given the familiarity of such not balancing among practicing teachers or teachers-in-training, we delve directly into noticing what balancing participation looks like. After establishing what that entails in the specifics of interaction, we then take a stab at promoting changes—through a set of changing exercises that help us work through what to look for, what to think about, and what to do in others' and one's own classes.

Noticing

As alluded to earlier, the kind of balancing we are talking about ultimately involves navigating between the vocal and the non-vocal, and relatedly, between the individual and the group. Such an act of balancing involves two broad sets of strategies, and we address each in turn below.

> **Strategies for balancing participation**: (1) shift focus away from the 'eager' individual without dismissing their contribution; (2) maintain focus on the 'struggling' individual without discouraging other volunteers.

Shift focus away from the 'eager' individual

How to keep the whole class in focus or on the same page at all times remains a constant challenge for the classroom teacher. Teachers often, for example, speak of not 'losing the class.' Any engagement with individual students, however, runs the exact risk of losing the class. One question, then, is how to disengage from individual students without dismissing their contribution. Skillful teachers achieve this delicate balance between the individual and the class in what seem to be entirely unremarkable ways. In the first segment below, the class has been working in small groups on a set of tongue twisters that involve difficult sound pairs such as /r/ versus /l/. As the segment begins, the teacher (TC) selects ST to read out aloud the first tongue twister, and he looks down at the handout during ST's reading (line 2).

(6) gaze shift to class [Waring & Carpenter, 2019]
```
01    TC:      go ahead ST.
02    ST:      f::ew (.) free (.) fruit (.) fli:es, fly (.) from. flames.
03    TC:      gaze up from handout with nod and extended arms to SS
04             pronunciation was ↑good?
05             (0.2)
06             pronunciation was good. now. what are the sou:nds.
07             that we're focusing on here.
```

Note that the teacher does two things in lines 03 & 04. He accepts the student's performance with the non-verbal gesture of nodding and the verbal assessment of *pronunciation was good*. At the same time, this acceptance combo is directed, via his gaze, not to the student individually, but to the entire class that is now being informed of the correct pronunciation of this particular tongue twister. Furthermore, this gaze shift has also paved the way for the teacher to re-engage the larger group, to which his follow-up question is addressed (lines 06 & 07). As such, the teacher appreciates the individual contribution while shifting focus back to the class.

A trickier task is disengaging from individuals who tend to take more than their fair share of the floor or who are what Erickson (2004) calls a 'turn shark' (also see Waring, 2013), and ST1 in the following segment is one such student. The class has just heard what is supposed to be a funny story on an audiotape, and the teacher is now asking how the story represents incongruity—an ingredient that engenders humor.

(7a) expected ending [Waring, 2014, p. 308]
01   TC: [okay:, (0.6) so:, how- how is this an example o:f incongruity.
                 [*to class*
02   (0.8)
03   according to what we heard in the introduction
04   [there's incongruity.   ]
05   ST1:   [very unexpected ending.]

Note that the teacher's initial invitation to reply directed towards the class is met with a (0.8) second silence. In line 03, he speaks again, reminding the class that there is indeed incongruity to be uncovered. Soon after he begins and before he finishes, however, we hear ST1's response of *very unexpected ending* (line 05). Knowing ST1's reputation as the class's 'turn shark,' what might the teacher do next?

(7b) expected ending [Waring, 2014, p. 308]
06   [(0.6)
                 [*TC looks to ST1*
07   TC: [so what's the expected ending.
                 [*points to ST1 but looks toward rest of class*
08   ST1:   that- (0.2)
09   ST2:   °it was silly ending. yeah.°
10   TC: *gestures for ST2 to continue*
11   ST2:   °it was unusual.°

As can be seen, in line 06, the teacher briefly looks towards ST1 during the (0.6) second silence, thereby acknowledging having heard her response, upon which he also builds his next question: *so what's the expected ending* (line 07), contrasting with ST1's *very unexpected ending* (line 05) while pointing to ST1. In multiple ways then, the teacher displays his recognition and appreciation of ST1's contribution. At the same time, however, he also makes sure that the next turn goes to someone other than ST1, and he does so by addressing this next question not to

ST1, but to the rest of the class (line 07). In one single turn then (line 07), the teacher manages to both include and exclude the individual who may pose a threat to even participation.

Observe that ST1 displays her understanding of the teacher's attempt by quickly cutting off what she started (line 08), and it is ST2's response, albeit delivered in a quiet voice (lines 09 & 11), that the teacher gesturally encourages (line 10). Thus, in this case, we see how the teacher efficiently and yet respectfully disengages from the talkative student so that unbalanced participation may be minimized.

Finally, disengaging from an individual student requires the teacher to make the split-second decision on when exactly such disengagement should begin, especially in cases where a student response may last longer than necessary and ends up occupying floor space that may be more productively allocated to others. In such cases, fine-grained monitoring of a student's developing talk is crucial. Prior to the following segment, the students have worked in groups to correct a list of sentences with typical language learner mistakes (e.g., misplacing/missing commas in non-restrictive relative clauses). The segment begins with the teacher's question of why even the best students would make these kinds of mistakes, and ST1 volunteers her answer in line 04 after a (2.2) second gap.

(8a) number one [Waring, forthcoming]
```
01    TC:    (lines omitted) why do you think (.) even the best students make
02           these mistakes. in essays. >why do you think.<
03           [(2.2)
             [TC scans the room
04    ST1:   and even though sometimes, >like when you-< you're sure
05           that you really know something?
06    TC:    nods
07    ST1:   then you just don't think, when you are writing?
08           [      a:nd      ] you just write.
09    TC:    [points and nods]
```

Note that ST1 begins answering in line 04. Upon the completion of her adverbial clause in line 05, TC nods in line 06, which may be a signal for ST1 to continue, which ST1 does in line 07 by producing the main clause of the sentence. She has by now offered at least one reason for why even the best students make these mistakes (i.e., *you just don't think when you're writing*), and her answer is possibly complete. The teacher appears to treat it as such with nodding as well as a pointing gesture (line 09), but ST1 continues at the same time by essentially repeating the idea of writing without thinking (*and you just write*), and this continuation can potentially extend even further (and it does, as shown below). What could the teacher do at this juncture to ensure that he can hear from others as well?

As can be seen, immediately following ST1's talk in line 08 in the prior portion of the segment, the teacher nods again, but notably, with his gaze shifted away from ST1 (line 11) while the latter continues (line 10).

(8b) number one [Waring, forthcoming]
```
10   ST1:     [            that's it.          ]
11   TC:      [nods with gaze shift away] nods
12            [ $NUmber one.$ ]
             [gaze back to ST1 with nods
13   ST1:     [ and you USUally ] don't check? °befo:re°
```

While the gaze-away nod (line 11) signals the initial move to disengage, the ensuing loud pronouncement of *NUmber one* delivered in a smiley voice appears to undo that disengagement, at least on the surface, as the teacher brings his gaze back to ST1 with nodding. In essence, however, by labeling ST1's contribution as *number one*, the teacher effectively treats her talk so far as complete and thereby closes it. At the same time, *number one* alludes to the possibility of other points to come, thus serving as an implicit invitation for others to contribute—another act of subtle disengagement. Still, ST1 continues and in fact does so competitively with raised volume (*USUally*)—in overlap with the teacher's *NUmber one*, offering a second reason (*and you usually don't check*) (line 13), which the teacher acknowledges and accepts but does so, as you may notice below, in a very specific way.

(8c) number one [Waring, forthcoming]
```
13   ST1:    [and you USUally] don't check? [°befo:re°]
14   TC:                                    [  .hhh.  ]
                                            [gaze away but points to S1
```

We may notice two things here. First, the large inbreath *.hhh* (line 14) signals that the teacher is gearing up to speak, and it is placed at the immediate completion of ST1's *and you usually don't check?* This precisely timed inbreath seems to pre-empt further continuation from the latter. As observed, ST1's next word *before* (line 13) is delivered in a quiet voice, and any further talk (e.g., *before submitting the work*) is abandoned thereafter. Second, along with the inbreath, the teacher points to ST1 while gazing away, thus exhibiting a dual orientation of attending and disengaging. This balancing act is carried out sequentially rather than simultaneously in the rest of the extract.

(8d) number one [Waring, forthcoming]
15   TC: [$which is a<u>no</u>ther problem.$
                [*gaze back to ST1*
16   [yes. number two. ST2.
                [*shifts gaze to ST2*
17   ST2:   for me:, when I need to (guess)? (continues)

Note that the teacher first accepts what ST1 offers as *another problem* and does so in a smiley voice as he gazes towards her. This is followed immediately with a shift of gaze away from ST1 towards ST2 whom the teacher verbally selects to offer *number two*.

Throughout this section, we have witnessed the teacher's constant efforts at moving away from the individual in caring, non-dismissive ways. This is largely accomplished by both verbal and non-verbal resources—and often simultaneously. As the teacher shifts his focus away from the individual, he takes great care to acknowledge, appreciate, and validate what the student has contributed so far. At times, for example, the same words accomplish the brilliant duality of conveying both endorsement and disengagement (e.g., *So what's the expected ending? Number one.*).

Maintain focus on the 'struggling' individual

Sometimes, balancing participation requires doing the opposite of shifting away from an individual, especially when that individual is someone who is less vocal and less likely to speak up in class. In such situations, the challenge is to carve out a space of participation for that particular individual in the midst of other eager volunteers. As you may notice, in order to avoid discouraging other volunteers, the teacher uses many of the strategies seen above. In the first extract below, the class is working on the meaning of 'produce' as a noun. As can be seen, ST1 is selected (line 04) but does not respond (line 05).

(9a) produce [Waring, 2013, pp. 330–331]
01   TC: I can tell <u>e</u>very single person in this class <u>does</u> know this word.
02   °you've all <u>seen</u> this wo:rd, in <u>s</u>upermarkets.°
03   (0.5)
04   [ST1?
                [*leans towards ST1*
05   (0.8)
06   [*hand extends to ST1*]
07   ST2:   [it's agricultural   ] products?

In line 06, the teacher persists in soliciting a response from ST1 by extending his hand towards her. At the same time, ST2 starts speaking and appears to be giving the correct response. What would you have done at this juncture as a teacher? We suspect that the easiest and most efficient move would be to accept the answer and move on. As will be seen, this is not what this teacher does in this case.

(9b) produce [Waring, 2013, pp. 330–331]

07	ST2:	it's agricultural
08		[products?]=
09	**TC:**	[ah- °yeah.°]
		[*to ST2 with finger up to 'on hold' position; pivots to pointing at 'yeah'*

Note that the teacher's initial reaction to ST2's response is to put it on hold. We hear the cut-off *ah* and see its accompanying upward finger. More importantly, this is done in overlap with ST2's *products* before she brings her response to its completion. As she does finish uttering *products*, however, we also see the teacher's gesture pivoting to a pointing one along with the affirming *yeah*. By delivering this *yeah* in a quiet voice after the 'on-hold' message, however, the teacher also sends the signal that he is treating ST2's response at this point as ancillary to the main course of action. Immediately thereafter, ST1, the selected student, begins speaking (line 10).

(9c) produce [Waring, 2013, pp. 330–331]

10	ST1:	=vege[tables]
11	**TC:**	[*gaze shift to ST1 with arm swerved to ST1*]
12	ST1:	a::n[d]
13	**TC:**	[A::]ND
		[*pivots to inducing gestures*
14	ST1:	°frui:t.°=
15	TC:	=[yes
		[*nods/retrieves arm/gazes away*

The teacher's gaze and arm swerve to ST1 upon hearing the first two syllables of her utterance. This is followed by an echoing *A::ND* in raised volume as the teacher encourages ST1 to continue with accompanying gestures (line 13). ST1's response is then completed and accepted in lines 14 & 15. The sequence does not end here. As shown below, the teacher returns to re-confirm what ST2 said earlier as acceptable (lines 17 & 18).

(9d) produce [Waring, 2013, pp. 330–331]
16   TC: <u>PRO</u>duce. >vegetables and fruits.<
17   [<u>o</u>r agricultural products
                     [*gazes and gestures to ST2*
18   [°like ST2 said.°
                     [to SS

In the above excerpt, the teacher maintains his focus on the selected student, who is a bit slow to respond, by persistently soliciting and encouraging her participation even as another student volunteers a correct answer. He is able to do so without discouraging the other student by quickly accepting and putting her response on hold and by re-affirming its acceptability later on. In so doing, he achieves a delicate balance between making room for the quiet students and ensuring that the other student's contribution is appreciated as well.

We now consider another example where the teacher manages to protect the space of a 'struggling' student while attending to other volunteering voices. The class is working on the 'so... that...' structure, and the segment begins with the teacher inviting ST1 to complete the sentence *New York is so multicultural that...* (lines 01 & 02). (Transcription note: empty parentheses = talk that cannot be clearly deciphered for transcription; $ = smiley voice; ° = quiet voice; > < = quickened pace.)

(10a) let her talk [Waring, 2013, pp. 331–332]
01   TC: ima:gine the sentence. New York is <u>so</u> multicultural tha:t,
02   *gestures out toward ST1*
03   (1.6)
04   ST2:   °(   )°
05   **TC:**   *holds up hand/nods/smiles to ST2*
06                 $°>just a second, just a second.<°$
07   (1.2)
08   tha<u>:</u>:t,

As shown, ST1 as the selected student does not respond during the (1.6) second long gap (line 03), after which ST2 begins talking (line 04). In response, the teacher does an on-hold hand gesture while smiling and nodding to ST2. This is followed by the quick and quiet *just a second, just a second* delivered in a smiley voice. While the 'stop' action momentarily hinders ST2's participation, the smiling and nodding as well as the hushed prosody softens the blow. We hear no further talk from ST2 thereafter (line 07), and the teacher repeats the final item of his initial solicitation with elongation and continuing intonation—again inviting its completion—which, again, someone other than ST1 provides (line 09).

(10b) let her talk [Waring, 2013, pp. 331–332]

```
09   ST3:    you never miss [your homeland.=
10   TC:                    [hand up to ST3 /nods/smiles
11   ST3:    =(                         )]
12   TC:     $just a second, let- let her try:$]
13   ST3:    sorry: hheh.
14   TC:     I know, we have so many wonderful people who wanna
             [ta:lk.]
15   ST1:    °[so:  ]
16           multicultural that uh we have many (  ) restaura:nts,°
```

In response to this second volunteer to complete the sentence, the teacher makes the more proactive move of cutting her off soon after she begins (line 10) but does so with the same verbally and visibly caring stance observed earlier (lines 10 & 12). This attempt to put ST3 on hold is upgraded with an explicit plea to *let her try* (line 12). ST3 responds to that plea with an apology coupled with a brief laugh (line 13). Rather than accepting the apology, however, the teacher in the next turn openly acknowledges the *wonderful people who wanna talk* (line 14), thus reframing ST3's action not as an infraction as suggested by the apology, but as a gesture to be embraced and welcomed. Perhaps as a result of the teacher's insistence on having her try, ST1 finally talks (lines 15 & 16). What happens next is also notable. As shown below, the teacher does not simply accept ST1's response and move on. He returns to the earlier volunteers (ST2 and ST3) and ensures that their voices are heard in their entirety as well (lines 17 & 19).

(10c) let her talk [Waring, 2013, pp. 331–332]

```
17   TC:     perfect, perfect. ST2. so multicultural tha:t,
18   ST2:    °(    )°
19   TC:     okay, ST3, go.
```

Clearly, the teacher is engaging in 'in the moment' micro-reflection by keeping in mind the need to return to ST2 and ST3 after ST1 speaks.

Thus, maintaining focus on the less vocal individual in the midst of other eager volunteers is not as simple as single-minded persistence in getting the individual to talk. In tandem with that avid focus is the need to remain undistracted by correct answers and attend to other voices in a timely, disciplined, and respectful manner.

In sum, an important aspect of balancing multiple demands in the language classroom involves balancing participation. Given the highly constrained time and space of this particular institutional context along with the teacher's limited attention resources, there is a constant tug-of-war between attending to the individual and the group, and between attending to this and that individual. How to create a classroom where everyone feels included within the various constraints remains an ongoing challenge for the practicing teacher. We have demonstrated two possible ways in which this can be achieved at the very micro-level of moment-to-moment interaction: (1) shift focus away from the individual in caring, non-dismissive ways and (2) maintain focus on the individual without discouraging other volunteers. Clearly, timing is of utmost importance. Executing the balancing act requires fine-grained monitoring of what students are saying word by word so that the proper action may be taken at the right time, be it disengagement (e.g., gaze away) or injunction (e.g., *just a second*). Also integral to this acrobatic balancing is the deployment of non-verbal means such as gaze and gesture as well as prosodic resources such as volume and pace. While gaze and gesture can efficiently send separate but simultaneous signals along with verbal messages without taking up substantive floor space (e.g., pointing to ST while addressing question to class; on-hold gesture to ST2 while focusing on ST1), prosodic packaging can make an otherwise disengaging move sound less off-putting (e.g., saying *just a second* in a quick and quiet voice). In addition, ingenious verbal designs alone can sometimes accomplish the duality of disengaging from one party and engagement with another (e.g., *Number one. So what's the expected ending?*). Finally, either maintaining or shifting focus would involve some party being placed on hold or moved to the sideline. To minimize the appearance of dismissing their participation, the teacher must handle the process with care and sensitivity—by quickly validating their contribution and right to contribute, and by giving them space at a later time.

Resources for Balancing Participation

(1) use words and gestures to encourage or discourage student talk as needed (e.g., nods, smiles, extended hand; index finger up)

(2) use words that multitask (e.g., *number one*)

(3) split words and prosody (e.g., say *just a second* in a quiet voice and quickened pace)

(4) split the verbal and non-verbal (e.g., positively assess the individual while gazing and turning to the group)

(5) split the body (e.g., point to the individual while gazing at the group)

(6) make explicit one's intention (e.g., *Let her finish. We have so many wonderful people who want to talk.*)

(7) make space for referencing and returning to on-hold responses

Changing

So far, we have focused on noticing what types of teacher conduct are conducive to balancing participation and what kinds of specific verbal and visible resources may be used to carry out the relevant conduct. While noticing serves as a prerequisite, and sets the stage, for changing, it does not automatically lead to change. A key component in our cycle of micro-reflection entails the work of instigating changes in one's conduct, and such work, as we argue, must be reflective in nature. As such, we offer a series of guided exercises to facilitate this reflective process of changing that moves from what to look for, to what to think about, and finally, to what to do.

What to look for

1. Based on your experiences as a student, a teacher, or an observer, what would you say might be three signs of balancing student participation? What would be some of the features of the student conduct in those situations, and what would be some of the features of the teacher conduct?

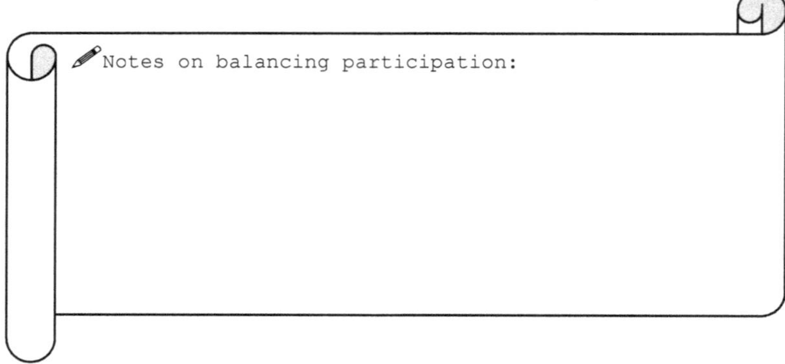

2. Consider the following extract taken from an adult ESL classroom, where ST1 is the one who tends to occupy more than her fair share of the floor. What does the teacher do (or not do) to balance participation?

(11) what is there to get [Waring, 2013, p. 843]

```
01   TC:   okay well, let's be laughter scientists for a moment,
02         and analyze (.) why do we have this reaction to the joke.=
03         or what is it um: (0.4) [  if we finish the joke  ]=
04   ST1:                         [It's kind of outrageous.]
```

```
05   TC:     =and [some]body said get it? (0.4)
06   ST1:          [ it's ]
07   TC:     what is there [to get.
08                         [quick slide nods to S1
09                [(0.3)
                  [TC scans class but not ST1
10   TC:     [ST2?
             [looks and gestures to ST2
```

What to think about

1. In our noticing section above, we have drawn attention to two strategies of balancing participation: disengaging from or maintaining focus on particular individuals. Focusing on the idea of balancing participation, think of any other strategies (positive or negative) based on your experiences and/or observations as a teacher or a student. Be as specific as possible in your description of the practice.
   (a) When is it done (e.g., initiating or responsive position), how is it done, and what response(s) does it receive?
   (b) What words, gestures, intonation, and timing are used in its delivery?
   (c) What alternatives are available at the time of its production?

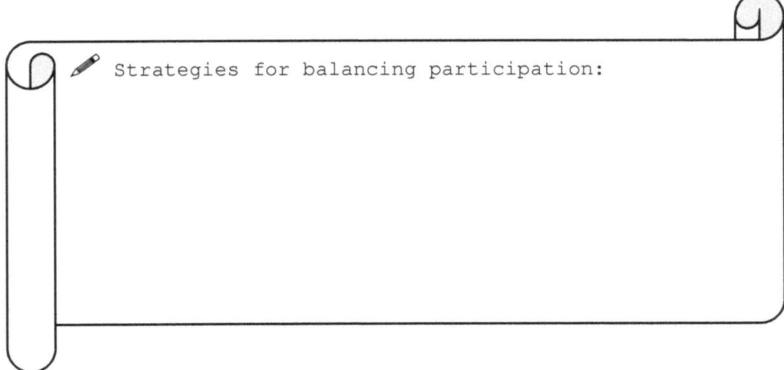

2. Consider the next two extracts taken from two different adult ESL classrooms. For each turn that the teacher takes in each extract, describe:
   (a) what alternatives there might be;
   (b) what he does precisely (e.g., X as opposed to Y);
   (c) what specific resources are used;

(d) in what way the teacher's conduct might be considered 'balancing participation';

(e) how it is responded to;

(f) what other choices there might be at this juncture to do 'balancing.'

(12) Japanese humor [Waring, 2014, p. 313]

```
01   TC:    [can you- can you feel any big differences betwee:n
             [to class
02          (.) say- (.) Am- American humor or English humor?
03   ST1:   yeah.
04   ST2:   mhm.
05   ST1:   well not- (0.2) I- I can feel it from Danish humor
06          °to° (.) to American.
07   TC:    yeah?
```

(lines omitted where ST1 talks)

```
08   ST1:   I think that's (0.2) you have to be careful with. °with that.°
09   TC:    okay. a'right, (0.2) [wha- what about- what about Japanese
                                  [to ST3 and ST4
10          humor.=uh (.) can y- can you say anything about
11          (0.2) differences between a (0.4)
12   ST3:   I don't know the difference.=but (0.2) ↑there is a
13          cartoon <South (.) Park,>
14   TC:    uh huh.
```

(13) this side over here [Waring, 2014, p. 314]

```
01   TC:    so, the farm was used (.) to: produ:ce (0.2) produce.
02          (1.0)
03          °or fruits.° ok↑ay.
04          (0.5)
05          >let's get someone< fro:m (0.5) [this side over here.=to do
                                            [gestures to left
06          number three.
07          who's brave.=over here to do number three.
08          ST1, you wanna try?
09   SS:    heh heh [heh
10   ST1:           [well-
11   TC:            [go ahea[d.   ]
12   ST1:                   [can] I- can I do the number four?
```

13   SS: [heh hhe heh heh hahahahhahahhaha hahh]
14   TC: [you wanna do number four? hahhahahha]
15   I̲'ll let you do number four then.=
16   okay, [okay.]
17   ST1:   [thank] you.

3.   In the next extract from another adult ESL classroom taken from Reddington (2018), the class is discussing music from different cultures. The teacher attempts to move to topic closure quite early in the extract while ST1 attempts to continue. At each teacher turn, consider the following:
     (a)   what the teacher could be doing at this particular juncture but is not;
     (b)   what she does instead;
     (c)   what interactional resources (verbal and visible) she uses to do what she does;
     (d)   in what way her choices might be demonstrating balancing student participation;
     (e)   how her conduct is received by the student;
     (f)   what other choices there might be at this juncture to do balancing.

(14) melody [Reddington, 2018, p. 9]
01   ST1:   it's: f̲aster or s̲lower melody, [dance,] it depends
02   TC: [mmm,]
                                           [*nods*

03   [°yeah.° [°yeah.°=
            [*shrugs.* [*nods*
04   ST1:   =with some s̲ongs,
05   TC: [°great.° *smiles*
             [*nods*
06   ST1:   about uh our u::h u:h n̲[ational,]
07   TC: [*nods*]
08   [°yeah.° *gaze ahead to SS* about the culture.
            [*nods*
09   [and maybe a little similar to Thai- telling the
            [*gaze/gesture to ST2*
10   [storie:s   [of your country.
            [*circling hand, nodding* [*gaze to ST1*
11   [okay. .hh
            [*gaze to side to whiteboard*

12   [a::nd going to <u>P</u>eru.
             [*gaze to ST3*
13   ST3:   well. Peru a:::h (0.4) is: (0.6) is a famous place in the world be-

What to do

1. Based on the skills you have developed so far, observe an actual lesson (with a video-camera if possible) with a specific focus on strategies to balance participation. Organize your notes using the following table.

Strategies for balancing participation	
Strategies	Details
1. 2. 3.	(a) What could have been done differently at this particular moment in the interaction? (b) What is not being done, and why? (c) What exactly is being done, and how? (d) How is what is being done taken up by the participants in the data?
Strategies for not balancing participation	
Strategies	Details
1. 2. 3.	(a) What could have been done differently at this particular moment in the interaction? (b) What is not being done, and why? (c) What exactly is being done, and how? (d) How is what is being done taken up by the participants in the data?

2. Repeat the same exercise above with a video-recording of your own teaching, and invite a colleague to either join the exercise or offer feedback on your own analysis.

3. With the observational materials you have gathered (video recordings preferably), identify moments where the teacher does balancing participation and try to work backwards to figure out what has been done to lead to that moment.

4. Try out specific practices of balancing participation in your own class one at a time. Make note of the effect of each in terms of specific student conduct. Make adjustments accordingly as you repeat the exercise.

Chapter 5

The FAB Classroom: Bringing It All Together

Even though categories can be useful tools for teaching and learning, real-life interactions almost never fit into neat boxes. Thus, while the FAB framework offers a way to describe and classify some of the kinds of actions that we believe lead to an engaging, democratic classroom, we hope that you have been questioning our choices as you have read this book. We certainly have! As we found examples for Chapters 2–4, we regularly asked ourselves and each other questions such as: 'Wait! Is this an example of fostering an inviting environment, or attending to student voices?' Or: 'Hmmm. Is this teacher balancing participation or balancing agendas?' The answer, in most cases, is 'Both.' In this chapter, we dig into that complexity, looking at three excerpts that highlight the ways in which the elements of our framework usually intersect in real time.

EXHIBIT I: TRADITIONAL DRUMS

Prior to the following extract taken from an adult ESL classroom, the teacher posed the question *What traditional music would you recommend that I listen to if I came to visit your country as a tourist?* (with the intended goal to provide 'conversation practice'; not shown) and had the students write their responses on the whiteboard. The students were then asked to speak about the responses, and ST1 took multiple turns and provided several details about Thai music. In other words, the teacher (TC) is now faced with the challenge of opening up opportunities to other students in the class.

(1) traditional drums [Reddington, 2018, p. 142]

```
01   ST1:    and they play with (.) u::h Thai::: (0.8) Thai musicians,
02   TC:     [mm hm,
             [smiles
03   ST1:    ↓yeah. like, (1.0) I don't know how to t-
```

04		how to:: [( )] [like

04   how to:: [(   )] [like
                                 [*mimes drumming*
05   TC: [yea-. I've se-]
                         [*smiles*
06   [yeah, with the different kinds of drums and
              [*mimes drumming*
07   [yeah] yeah yeah.
08   ST1:   [yeah.]
09   [(   )]
10   TC: [yeah yeah. traditional musi-
              [*nods*
11   yeah yeah yeah. [traditional] drums.
12   ST1:   [traditional.]
13   TC: [yeah.
              [*nods; gaze to whiteboard*
14   traditional instruments.
15   [°okay.°   [yeah. good. ↑thank you. all right.
              [*gaze to ST1* [*gestures to ST1*
16   [we're gonna go to <u>Slo</u>vakia.
              [*gaze to ST2*
17   *quick gaze to board and back to ST2*
18   which I would love to do, espe[cially (continues)
                                            [*gaze to board*

Task 1

Take a few minutes to read through the transcript above and act it out with a partner if possible. Ignore the non-verbal markings first. Then, start adding the non-verbal to your reading once you feel you have gotten a good handle on just what is being said. Rehearse as many times as you would like to get a feel for the interaction. Next, try to identify precisely what the teacher does to solve this 'participation' problem in the moment. Tie each of your observations with a specific line number(s).

As Reddington (2018) notes in her analysis, a 'package' of practices is routinely used by the teacher to gracefully exit interaction with individual students who may be speaking a bit too much and open up the floor for others: (1) *validate contribution*; (2) *pre-empt further participation*, and (3) *bind contributions* (by drawing connections between the current and other student contributions). These practices may be implemented in different ways using a variety of resources. Validating, for example, can be done through such obvious moves as positive assessments or by providing further evidence for the point being made. Pre-empting can be accomplished explicitly by saying 'I'm going to stop you right here' or through more implicit means. By the same token, binding need not always come in the form of 'What you just said is connected to what X said before.' Learning to recognize the various ways of (or resources for) implementing a particular practice in actual interaction is part and parcel of developing our 'professional vision' (Goodwin, 2018) of being a teacher.

Task 2

Consider the same transcript again, and identify specific teacher talk and behavior (point to the specific line numbers) that would exemplify the three practices:
(1) validating: ____
(2) pre-empting: ____
(3) binding: ____

Taking stock of the validating moves made by the teacher, we see a great deal of nodding and smiling throughout the sequence. More specifically, we see her uttering the continuer *mm hm* (Schegloff, 1982) in line 02 while smiling despite ST1's disfluency in line 01, and we also see her chiming in in line 05 as ST1 displays difficulty explaining the type of activities Thai musicians engage in, doing what is referred to in conversation analysis as progessional overlap (Jefferson, 1983) to propel the forward movement of the sequence. By saying *yea- I've see-* while smiling, the teacher attempts to offer support for what ST1 is striving to articulate but halts her talk as ST1 continues. The teacher only resumes speaking after ST1's miming of drumming, where he clearly indicates a need for verbal support, which the teacher promptly provides in line 06 with *yeah, with the different kinds of drums* while echoing ST1's gesture of miming. Here, validating is achieved through both the gestural repeat and the verbal affirmation of drumming. Finally, messages of validating are also sent through such brief tokens of affirmation and appreciation as *yeah*, *good*, and *thank you* in line 15.

Along with all this support for ST1's contribution, are there any indications at all in this extract of the teacher pre-empting his contribution? Nothing as explicit as 'Let me stop you right there' for sure. There are, however, subtle signals of the teacher showing her stance that there is no need for ST1 to engage in any further explication. In line 05, her confirming attempts of *yea- I've se-* can potentially render ST1's struggle to explain unnecessary. In line 07, the multiple saying of *yeah yeah yeah* has been documented in the CA literature as a resource for signaling to a co-participant that they have persisted unnecessarily (Stivers, 2004), and it seems to be performing the same function here. Notice that *yeah yeah yeah* is produced in lieu of continuing with the *and* in line 06. There is, in other words, a clear shift from further developing the topic of Thai music to moving towards topic closure. In addition, even as ST1 continues (line 09), the teacher persists in her overlapping talk (lines 10 & 11) with further tokens of (multiple) *yeah*, which treats ST1's continuation as non-news (as opposed to, for example, 'oh'). Other clearer signals of closing include the gaze to the white board in line 13 that suggests more items to come, the *okay* delivered in a quiet tone in line 15 that alludes to some sort of winding down, and some classic pre-closings items as *good*, *thank you*, and *all right* (Button, 1987, 1990).

Also integral to what Reddington (2018) refers to as the graceful exit is binding contributions, as the teacher makes connections between the various contributions. Her reference to *traditional* drums and instruments (lines 11 & 14), for example, harkens back to her original question soliciting sharing of traditional music that binds all contributions. She also does binding by referencing Slovakia (which has its own traditional music) and gazing towards ST2 who is responsible for its sharing (line 16) as well as the corresponding item on the board (line 17). By momentarily bringing these connections to the foreground, the teacher manages to remind the students of the larger picture to which the class is to return and to which ST1's contribution belongs. As such, she offers an account for taking the floor from ST1 while including her in the larger enterprise at the same time.

Having now considered the package of practices used by the teacher to manage the very delicate situation of ensuring both extended and even participation, you might already have developed the sense that what the teacher does exemplifies all the components of FAB that we have been illustrating throughout this book.

Task 3

Reread and re-enact (if you're working with someone) the transcript one more time. Specify the teacher's ways of achieving FAB. Again, point to the specific line number(s) with each of your observations.

(1) Foster an inviting environment: _______________________________

(2) Attend to learner voices: ___________________________________

(3) Balance competing demands: _________________________________

As you might have noticed, all of the validating moves noted earlier contribute to **fostering an inviting environment.** These include such tokens of affirmation such as nodding, smiling, appreciation, positive assessment, gestural repeats, and invitation for continuation. Also contributing to **fostering an inviting environment** is showing the student that you understand exactly what they are struggling to articulate (as opposed to a simple 'huh?', for example) and offering the precise help they need to complete that articulation. More importantly, it is the precise timing of these tokens and displays as attentive responses to the student's contribution that render them 'inviting.' A delayed *mm hm* after line 01, for example, would give off a very different feel from the one placed immediately after ST1's utterance in line 01.

Likewise, timing is central to the craft of attending to learner voice, with the uttering of *mm hm* in line 02 as our very first example. Note that in line 01, ST1 displays difficulty completing the clause *and they play with* and restarts with an elongated *Thai*. A (0.8) second pause ensues before he restarts with *Thai* and delivers the complete noun phrase *Thai musicians* in continuing intonation. The teacher's *mm hm* with smiles is placed precisely after this successful self-repair, indicating her close monitoring of ST1's turn so far and displaying her understanding that his turn is yet to be completed. The same *mm hm* would not work to show attending in line 05, for example, where the student has just explicitly expressed his difficulty (*I don't know how to*). At this juncture, rather than letting ST1 to continue his struggle, the teacher attempts to validate what ST1 is trying to express with her own experience. In fact, her attending is so fine-tuned that she immediately halts her attempt upon noticing ST1's continuation. The next instance of attending may be observed in line 06 as the teacher promptly offers the verbal animation of ST1's miming of drumming along with a gestural repeat of the mime.

With regard to balancing multiple demands, an obvious observation is that the entire episode showcases how the teacher balances even an extended participation. In addition, we see various types of balancing accomplished in minute details throughout the extract. The halted attempts in line 05 show her delicate dancing within a split second to offer help, to try to close the sequence so others can contribute, and to let ST1 continue when he does. The affirming (multiple) *yeah*'s similarly validate ST1's contributions while at the same time signaling that no further explication is necessary. Finally, producing the final *yeah* in line 13 while nodding and gazing to the whiteboard solidifies the teacher's alignment with ST1's contribution on the one hand and hints at the need for others to contribute on the other.

Task 4

Return to the same extract one last time. Consider the teacher's turns beginning in lines 02, 05, 10, and 13. Think of two sets of alternatives that may be exercised during those slots: (1) what could be said or done to embody the opposite of FAB, and (2) what could be said or done to bring about FAB in ways other than what is shown in the transcript. As you play out the various scenarios, try to include what the students' responses/reactions would be following the various choices.

EXHIBIT II: SCHOLARSHIP

In this fairly extended stretch of interaction from an adult ESL classroom, the teacher has asked students to work in pairs to find out what makes each other *different* or *special*, and we join the interaction when the teacher asks Jia to share with the class her discoveries about Pia. We will break this long episode into four smaller installments and work through them bit by bit.

(2a) scholarship [Boblett, 2020]
```
01    TC:     what did you find out about Pia.
02            what makes her (0.5) [different. °special.°]
03    Jia:                         [      uh:::::::::    ] Pia?
04            she: lived in NYC for four months,
05    TC:     nods
06    Jia:    [because of uh::: [schola?
            [gaze to Pia      [gaze to T
07    TC:     .h a [°sch↓olarship.°=
                  [widened eyes with a downward nod
08    Jia:    =yes [scholarship.]
09    TC:         [ °isn't it.° ] a scholarship.
                 [picks up chalk +nods
10    Jia:    °yeah.°
```

Task 5

Take a few minutes to read through the transcript above and act it out with a partner if possible. Ignore the non-verbal markings first, and start adding those markings to your reading and acting once you feel you have gotten a good handle on just what is being said. Rehearse as many times as you would like to get a feel for the interaction. Then, try to locate any FAB elements you can find in this brief interaction. What does the teacher do to **foster an inviting environment, attend to learner voices,** and **balance competing demands?** Finally, think about what possibly could or should happen after line 10.

You might have noticed the teacher's *nods* in line 05—a simple gesture that indicates that Jia is on the right track and invites her to continue. An inviting environment is built bit by bit through gestures as small as a nod. A clear instance of 'attending' can be found in line 07 when the teacher promptly provides verbal assistance after Jia's display of difficulty as she searches for and is unable to complete the word 'scholarship' while turning her gaze towards the teacher—an implicit solicitation for help (line 06). A little balancing act may also be seen in the specific manner in which *scholarship* is offered as assistance (line 07). The prosodic (word stress in conjunction with quiet voice and lowered pitch after an inbreath) and gestural (widened eyes with a downward nod) qualities of the delivery converge to register the word as 'special.' As such, at the same time as the teacher provides carefully tailored individual assistance to Jia, she also signals to the entire class (including Jia) 'scholarship' as a noticeable language item that perhaps warrants further attention, as evidenced in her subsequent gesture of picking up the chalk—a pre-instruction move (line 09). This is a juncture where perhaps a natural instinct for many of us is to let Jia return to her telling, but that is not a choice that the teacher makes in this particular case. We get a sense of whether that is a worthwhile choice as the segment develops. As seen below, the teacher begins checking the class's understanding of the word 'scholarship,' and at least at a first glance, it does not seem to be a problematic word.

(2b) scholarship [Boblett, 2020]

11	TC:	[>do you know how to spell that?< you know what that is?
		[*looks around room and gets up from chair*
12	Cla:	yes.
13	TC:	[>do you know what a schola-<
		[*turns to Clara's side of room*

14	Cla:	*nods*
15	TC:	[>yes? you know what a [scholar]ship is?<=
		[*points to Clara* [*pivots pointing to Ana next to C*
16	Cla:	[*nods*]
17	Ana:	=[°yeah.°]
18	TC:	°yeah,↓Ana you know.°
19		[scholarship?
		[*slow scan with pointing hand around room and stops at Mas*
20	Mas:	*vigorous nods*
		[*continues with large nods*]
21	TC:	[>do you know what that is?<]
		[*quickly pivots gaze and gesture to Di who sits next to Mas*
22		<u>Di</u>, a do you know what a scholar[ship is?]
23	Di:	[>I̲ don't] know.<
24	TC:	=[explain that. to (.) °°to Di what that is.°°
		[*turns to Jia*

> **Task 6**
>
> Repeat the procedures earlier: Take a few minutes to read through the transcript above, and act it out with others if possible. Ignore the non-verbal markings first, and start adding those markings to your reading once you feel you have gotten a good handle on just what is being said. Rehearse as many times as you would like to get a feel for the interaction before answering the following question: What exactly is the teacher trying to do in these few lines, and how is she doing that? Are there any elements of FAB that you can identify? What would you have done differently at the teacher's turns in lines 13, 15, 18, 21, and 24?

Checking understanding appears to be the teacher's business here, and she does so thoroughly and methodically as she moves from one student to another utilizing both verbal and visible means. Verbally, we hear her repeated deployment of *Do you know X? You know X*. Visibly, we see her using gaze, gesture, and body to scan the room as she moves, stops, and pivots. The teacher could have stopped at hearing the very first *yes* in line 12, but she didn't. One might argue that what is being incrementally built here is an environment that invites—a sense that 'everybody matters' and that 'no one should be left behind' in this joint endeavor of learning, where spaces are carved out for all participants to have their concerns voiced and voices heard. As shown, Jia is selected as the explainer of 'scholarship' to Di in lieu of a teacher explanation that might have been a more expedient choice. In addition, what we have referred to as 'attending to learner voice' may be observed in the very small detail of how she turns to Clara's side of the room immediately upon hearing her *yes* response in line 12. Finally, balancing multiple demands does not appear to figure prominently in this stretch of interaction. We now turn to what happens next.

(2c) scholarship [Boblett, 2020]

```
25   Jia:    °uh:::::: [ scholarship  ] (.) is like uh:° (0.8) when we:: (2.0)
26   TC:               [<°if you can.°]
27   Jia:    do: >graduation?<
28   TC:     [(0.8)
             [TC crosses arms, one hand to chin
29           okay, [after-       ] [after we gra]duate?
30   Jia:          [after gradua-] [°after gra-° ]
31           after we graduate?
32   Jia:    we: receive (0.8) [$s(h)ometh(h)ing hehhehheh$ .HHH
                               [turns to T and gestures 'frame'
33   TC:     ↑ah: (.) you receive a: like [a diploma=
                                          [gestures rectangle
34           =>or something I think it's a< li:ttle bit d↓ifferent
35           [than that?]
36   Jia:    [ oh really?]
37           I think.
```

Task 7

Repeat the procedures earlier: Take a few minutes to read through the transcript above, and act it out with a partner if possible. Ignore the non-verbal markings first and start adding those markings to your reading once you feel you have gotten a good handle on just what is being said. Rehearse as many times as you would like to get a feel for the interaction before answering the following question: What elements of FAB may be observed? What are some of the possible alternatives at the teacher's turns in lines 26, 28, and 33?

Note that immediately upon hearing Jia's *uh:::::* delivered in a quiet voice, the teacher quickly adds to her initial directive in a quiet tone *if you can* that gives Jia's option to not go on. Such quick adjustment shows the very first sign of 'attending' in this brief extract. The teacher then further attends in line 29 by building on Jia's turn, reformulating her *when we do graduation* (lines 25 & 27) into *after we graduate*. Then again, in response to Jia's gesturing of 'frame,' the teacher promptly offers *diploma* as the verbal representation of the 'frame' gesture—precisely what Jia is striving to articulate with the laughter-interpolated *something*. Notably, this is done despite the fact that Jia's explication of 'scholarship' is now clearly not on the right track. The teacher's priority at the moment is not the correct answer but offering maximal assistance to Jia as she works through her mini-language problem.

Immediately thereafter, however, we obtain a glimpse into the balancing act the teacher is trying to pull off within the same turn. As shown in line 34, she rushes to complete the current utterance with *or something* and, without a pitch drop, begins the new utterance with *I think....* In other words, there is a sense that providing the word 'diploma' as sought by Jia is as important as what is coming up next. What we hear next is the teacher's feedback on Jia's explanation of 'scholarship' as 'diploma.' Rather than treating it as completely wrong, however, she uses the phrase *a little bit different* with stress, elongation, lowered pitch, and regular pace, all of which combine to give off a sense of deliberate wording that draws attention to this assessment, and in particular, its mitigating quality. In other words, *a little bit* is now hearable as a cautiously toned-down version of an assessment that clearly informs Jia of her less-than-ideal explanation of 'scholarship' but is at the same time framed, not punitively, but as an invitation for small adjustments—one that contributes to **fostering an inviting environment**. With a single teacher turn then, we see two sorts of balancing here: balancing the student's agenda to find the word for 'diploma' and the teacher's agenda to elicit a definition of 'scholarship,' and balancing the need to control the pedagogical content and that of maximizing participation. What happens next offers further dosages of FAB.

(2d) scholarship [Boblett, 2020]
38   TC: what can we add to [that.=
                         [*gaze to Ana and away*
                       [*turns to group; hands still pointing to Jia*
39   Ana: [°°yeah.°°   =yeah.=
40   TC: =let's add more inform[ation to that=
                             [*turns to Jia and points*
41   =because it's connected to school.
42   Jia: mhm?
43   TC: absolutely right. *gaze shifts to one side of room*
44   [it's connected to a school.
             [*holds 'palm' gesture and starts moving slowly to Ana side of room*

```
45   Ana:   °uh yeah°
46   TC:    [but wha-        [what-        [help us (  )-]
            [inducing gesture [turns to Ana
47   Ana:                    [°yeah.°       [if you are ve]ry very
48          good at school, and you apply: [at the (.) college,
49   TC:                                    [nods and points to Pia
50   Jia:   mm::::
51   TC:    [if you are very very good at school.
            [points to Pia while shifting gaze between P and J with smile
52          [gaze back to Ana with nods]
53   Ana:   [  yeah? you- you apply to  ] college?
54   Jia:   mhm?
55   Ana:   the college wi:ll give you: .hh recognize [you=
                                                      [turns to TC
56          =[so:me
             [turns to Jia then back to TC
57   Jia:   money?=
58   Di:    =the mo[ney?       ]
59   TC:           [↓↑AH:] they wi:ll (0.5) [they will give you:
                   [turns to class          [mimes throwing money to P
60          >they will give you< mon↑ey?
61   SS:    [(loud chatter and laughter)
62   TC:    [money, (  ) money? money?
            [mimes counting out money
```

Task 8

Repeat the procedures earlier: Take a few minutes to read through the transcript above, and act it out with others as students if possible. Ignore the
non-verbal markings first, and start adding those markings to your reading
once you feel you have gotten a good handle on just what is being said.
Rehearse as many times as you would like to get a feel for the interaction
before answering the following question: What elements of FAB may be
observed? Ground your observation in specific line numbers, and describe
the precise verbal and visible resources engaged in each case. Also consider
what some of the possible alternatives might be at each of the teacher turns.

We know that prior to this segment, the teacher has just made it clear that 'scholarship' is not exactly 'diploma.' Line 38 is a place where she could explain what it actually is. Instead, she adds the epistemic downgrader *I think* in response to Jia's news-marking *oh really?*, thus momentarily adopting a stance of uncertainty that is conducive to opening up a space for participation (Creider, 2016). As it turns out, this is indeed what she proceeds to do as she turns to the class and invites the collective *we* to *add to that* (line 38) while still pointing to Jia. With this ensemble of verbal and visible means, the teacher builds what is now a joint endeavor to solve the 'scholarship' problem. An inviting environment is thus being fostered not only by validating Jia's initial attempt but also by including everyone as potential contributors to the project. At the same time, by inviting the class to *add*, the teacher also 'attends' to Jia's initial contribution by building on rather than bypassing or rejecting it. Furthermore, insofar as this invitation to add validates and encourages participation on the one hand and ensures the development of substantive understanding on the other, one might argue that she is also balancing multiple demands.

Similar observations may be made throughout the rest of the extract, and we only highlight a few here. In line 41, the teacher does more work to ensure that Jia is encouraged rather than discouraged for her initial attempt. As shown, the teacher appends her invitation to *add* with an account starting with *because*, further specifying what is valid in Jia's initial contribution as she turns and points towards Jia. This is followed by the resounding endorsement *absolutely right* (lines 43) following Jia's own acknowledgment. We also see the teacher moving towards Ana's side of the room in line 44. Recall that Ana is the very first to say *yeah* when the teacher says 'scholarship' is *a little bit different* from 'diploma' and the very first to respond when the teacher asks *what can we add to that* (line 39), at which point the teacher very briefly establishes gaze with her. The moving toward Ana in line 44 is not a random occurrence but a 'return' of sorts. It seems as if the teacher had momentarily put on hold the initial recognition of Ana as the next speaker (line 38) in order to offer Jia further validation (line 41). Within these quick few seconds of oscillating between Jia and Ana then, we also see the fine-tuned balancing work the teacher is doing. One final point we would like to draw your attention to is the beautiful choreography that may be observed in line 51. The verbal repetition of *if you're very very good at school* attends to Ana's contribution so far by implicitly accepting it; the 'smiley' pointing to Pia alludes to the latter's achievement as a scholarship recipient; the shifting gaze between Pia and Jia now designates Jia (whose initial attempt needs further work) as the recipient of Ana's added explication. We see and feel an inviting environment because each single moment is made relevant to the class as a collective whole, where each participant is attended to for their unique presence, and in this breathtakingly complex environment, balancing multiple demands is not a luxury, but a must.

EXHIBIT III: SILENT BUTTERFLIES

Our final extract takes place in the same bilingual French-English kindergarten we have visited in earlier chapters. This interaction starts first thing in the morning, when the children and teachers are about to start cleaning up for circle time. In this school, each class is named after an insect. This class is known as the 'papillons,' or butterflies. In line 01, we see one of the two teachers, TC1, talking to the other teacher (TC2) about whether the 'papillons' can go to their places for circle time and wait quietly for their classmates to finish getting ready. This extended transcript is divided into four sections below. (Transcription note: In this transcript, each letter 'C' in the non-verbal marking stands for one clap, and each 'K' stands for one slap to the knees.)

(3a) silent butterflies [Creider, 2016]
01   TC1:   I'd like to try if the papillons, can
02   <wai>t in their place, sh: for morning circle,
03   while the other children clean up (0.2) I
04   wonder if they can do it. TC2?
05   TC2:   what?
06   TC1: $I'm not su:re$ that if they can do it,
07   TC2:   do what?=
08   TC1:   [*circling finger in air, gaze at T2*]
            [=<to wait,   ] *points to rug* in
09   their place, > while the other children
10   finish- [*circling gesture towards T2*]
11   TC2:   [silently you mean?   ]
12   TC1:   [*turns away from TC2, walks towards back table*
            [*silently.*
13   TC2:   *whistles* [*continuing to work on clay at table, gaze down*
14   [that's a bit of a challenge. it's
15   [more for first grade, =   ]
16   Oliver: [*sitting down next to Jake. smiles at Jake*]
17   TC2:   [*smiles   *]
            =[no?   ](0.4) [huh. (0.2)]
            we'll see.=

```
18   Jake:    [finger to lips, gaze at Oliver.]( )
19   TC2:     =looks towards TC1.
20   Oliver:  [gaze straight ahead, puts hands in lap
21   TC1:     [we'll see.
22   Frank:   [sitting cross-legged on rug.
              [C C C
23   TC2:     [gaze back at table          ]
              [you need a lot of- of exercises-] alot of: of-
24            of meditat [ion for that.]
25   Frank:              [C K       ] C K K C K K C C
```

Task 9

Take a few minutes to read through the transcript above, and act it out with a partner if possible. Ignore the non-verbal markings first, and start adding those markings to your reading once you feel you have gotten a good handle on just what is being said. Rehearse as many times as you would like to get a feel for the interaction. Then, try to locate any FAB elements you can find in this brief interaction. What does the teacher do to **foster an inviting environment, attend to learner voices**, and **balance competing demands?** Finally, think about what could or should happen after line 25.

You may have noted that TC1 and TC2 are very clear, which is one way to **foster an inviting environment.** For younger students, especially, it can be stressful to guess what a teacher wants them to do. We notice, then, that TC1 does not say something general, such as 'It's time for morning circle.' Instead, she and TC2 describe the specific set of actions *wait in their place* (line 02) *while the other children clean up* (line 03) *silently* (line 11). TC1 even points exactly to the 'place' in question in line 08. At the same time, the teachers are treating this subject lightly, even humorously. Rather than giving a series of orders to students, the teachers speak to each other, pretending that they don't know if the papillons are capable of such a 'challenge' (line 14). Note TC2's smile in line 17 and TC1's smiley voice in line 06, both of which show the joking tone of this interaction. This use of humor is one way to **balance competing demands,** since it allows the teachers to give a set of orders, while also attending to their students' need to be treated as competent, or as someone who is an independent agent.

We can also note that at least one student takes his teachers' challenge seriously. In line 16, Oliver sits down next to Jake on the rug and smiles at him. Rather than responding with his own smile, or—more likely—starting a conversation, Jake puts his fingers to his lips, the gesture for silence. Oliver responds to his friend by putting his hands carefully in his lap, and looking straight ahead.

But then, in line 22, even as TC2 and TC1 are continuing their joking conversation with each other, something new happens. Frank sits down cross-legged on the rug, thus following the first part of his teachers' directions. He starts to clap his hands together, and then begins a pattern of claps and knee slaps (line 25). Have you thought about how TC2 and TC1 might respond to this? It is an interesting action on the part of Frank. He *is* following directions, in the sense that he is sitting in his place. As for whether he is being quiet, that depends upon our definition of the term. He is not talking, or otherwise directly engaging with his classmates, but he is using his body to make at least some noise. Let's see how his teachers respond:

(3b) silent butterflies [Creider, 2016]

26	**Oliver:**	**waves floppy hands in front of body**
		[C C K, almost in rhythm w/ Frank
27	Frank:	[C C K *continues, almost in rhythm w/ Oliver*
28	**TC2:**	***turns to look at rug* what's happening? ooh la**
29		**la they can- ah::**
30	Rose:	*sits on rug*
31	Jake, Rose:	*join clapping game*
32	Elaine:	*joins*
33	**TC2:**	**what's happening [Hana? (.) are] you ok?**
34	S?:	[ayiya]
35	Hana:	*nods*
36	**TC2:**	**si- silently we said.**
37	Ilse:	*sits down, joins game*
38	Becca:	*sits down, settles skirt*
39	**TC2:**	**[*gets up and walks off camera***
		[can you please clean up now? I need the
40		**table.**
41	Becca:	*joins game*
42	**TC1:**	**[*walking through room, arranging chairs***
		[that's not bad,=

> **Task 10**
>
> Repeat the procedures earlier: Take a few minutes to read through the tran-
> script above, and act it out with others as students if possible. Ignore the
> non-verbal markings first, and start adding those markings to your reading
> once you feel you have gotten a good handle on just what is being said.
> Rehearse as many times as you would like to get a feel for the interaction
> before answering the following question: What elements of FAB may be
> observed? Ground your observation in specific line numbers, and describe
> the precise verbal and visible resources engaged in each case. Also consider
> what some of the possible alternatives might be at each of the teacher turns.

Although our focus throughout this book has been on teacher actions, we can
also think about how our students are skillfully navigating the competing demands
of classroom life. We noted earlier that Frank was both following his teachers'
directions *and* starting a new trajectory of his own. And, it is interesting to watch
how this trajectory plays itself out. In line 26, we see Oliver start to make his own
set of movements, as he waves his hands in front of his body. This movement then
morphs into a series of claps and slaps. As the two children begin to move in concert, TC2 turns to look at them, asking *what's happening?* (lines 28 & 33). She then
says *ooh la la* (remember that this is a French-speaking classroom!). This expression
of surprise serves two purposes, as it simultaneously shows appreciation for the
student actions TC2 is witnessing, and also puts TC2 in the position of someone
who can be surprised, someone who is a co-learner in the classroom. Thus, we see a
teacher **fostering an inviting environment** *and* **attending to learner voice** in this
moment. (We can note that 'voice' does not necessarily mean 'speaking,' but can
also refer to physical actions on the part of learners!)

Throughout the next few lines, more and more students join into the game that
Frank created (lines 31, 32, 37, 38, & 41). Finally, we see TC1 acknowledge their
actions. As she physically attends to the classroom environment, by pushing chairs
towards tables (line 42), she tells the students that *that's not bad* (line 42). This is
an interesting move. On the one hand, TC1 is being open, and thus **fostering an
inviting environment**. At the same time, she positions herself as the teacher here,
or the person who is allowed to tell students, literally, if their actions are permissi-
ble (or 'not bad'), thereby **balancing competing demands**. What do you think she
does next? Let's look.

(3c) silent butterflies [Creider, 2016]

43	TC1:	=[if you do that with control you can do it
		[*3 rhythmic downward motions with palms*
44		*arranging objects on a table.*

(Lines omitted: teachers discussing clean up with students who are not on the rug, and making plans with each other)

45	S?:	ah oo ah oo oo
46	TC1:	sh::::
47	Paul	*hitting ground in front of knees with more force*
48	Claire:	*hitting ground in front of knees strongly*
49	Ss?:	oh ai ai
50	TC2:	eh [oh:::::] that started out well
51	TC1:	[oh:::::] you started off well, it's true *walking towards circle*
52		[*sitting down at one end of the circle*
		[now it's setting off. we're going to sit down::
53		not ba::d. who had the idea to [make gestures=
54	Frank:	[K K K...
55	TC1:	=like that?
56	Frank:	[me.
		[*raises hand*
57	Ilse, Na:	*raise hands*
58	TC1:	who started that. that wasn't bad because you
59		could move, but it wasn't very:: uh you didn't
60		make a lot of noise, and uh: you could do some
61		thing while: while waiting. so do you think that
62		it's a good activity to do while you wait? *K K K throughout*
63	Ss:	yes::: [:]
64	TC1:	[ye]s I agree >do you agree TC2?
65	TC2:	yes yes yes. I found that you were u[h: XX]
66	TC1:	[but we]
67		don't do this *leans forward and pats rug loudly*
68		[that makes too much noise. ok?]
		[*sits up, shakes finger in front of body*] K K K...

Task 11

Repeat the procedures earlier: Take a few minutes to read through the transcript above, and act it out with others as students if possible. Ignore the non-verbal markings first, and start adding those markings to your reading once you feel you have gotten a good handle on just what is being said. Rehearse as many times as you would like to get a feel for the interaction before answering the following question: What elements of FAB may be observed? Ground your observation in specific line numbers, and describe the precise verbal and visible resources engaged in each case. Also consider what some of the possible alternatives might be at each of the teacher turns.

We ended the last section just as TC1 had told the students that their new game was *not bad*, and we now see that she tells them *you can do it*. Even more interesting, though, are the teacher's visible actions here. Notice that as she speaks, she is making rhythmic downward gestures with her hands, almost as if she were hitting her own knees (she is standing up at this point). It is as if she is joining in the game, at the same time as she comments on it. She is quite literally following her students' lead, which is one way of **attending to learner voice.** The next 28 lines, which we do not include here, in order to save space, are worth mentioning: The teachers simply go about their own work, discussing plans for the day, and helping students who are not yet on the rug to clean up. Throughout this time, the students on the rug continue to play their clapping game. The very fact that the teachers do not acknowledge the game is a way of fostering student independence, or **fostering an inviting environment.** But then, in lines 45 through 49, something starts to change. Remember back at the beginning of this extract, when TC1 and TC2 wondered if students could sit *quietly*? Both sitting and remaining quiet seem to become difficult for these kindergartners. In lines 45 and 49, we hear students start to punctuate their clapping game with more noisy yelling. And, in lines 47 and 48, two students start to lean forward out of their places, hitting the ground in front of them with more force. There are so many ways that the teachers could respond to this. One possibility is to simply ignore the rising noise level. Another would be to shut the game down and tell everyone to stop. Or, a third possibility would be to directly tell students to 'quiet down.'

What do our teachers choose? A different option. They acknowledge the noise level non-verbally—with both teachers choosing an elongated 'oh' to start turns (lines 50 and 51). More importantly, they then accentuate the positive, both of them telling students that they 'started off well.' By focusing on what students have done well, the teachers **foster an inviting environment**. Or, to put it differently, the teachers are **balancing competing demands** by attending simultaneously to the rising noise level *and* to the students' sense of independence. We see TC1 do similar work a few lines later, when she asks the students if *they* think it's a 'good idea' to play this game while they wait for morning meeting to begin. First, though, she returns to her original instructions, as she tells students that this game allows them to move and not make too much noise. Then, by asking for their opinion, she positions them as independent, thus **fostering an inviting environment**. And, we can also notice that as she speaks, TC1 continues to softly slap her knees (line 62), as if she were joining the game! This non-verbal action is a subtle way of following a student lead, or **attending to learner voice**.

DISCUSSION

In sum, in this chapter, we have tried to highlight the many different ways that teachers can bring together our three guiding principles. As you reflect on your own teaching and the teachers you observe, we hope you begin to notice moments when teachers attend to multiple elements of the framework simultaneously. And following the cycle of micro-reflection, such noticing should lead to changes in your own practice. As you have probably gathered by now, we believe that 'micro' moments in the classroom can have major impact. As Farrell (personal communication, August 30, 2019) notes, 'each river starts with one drop!' We hope, via the transcripts, exercises, and descriptions in this book, to have offered a series of concrete tools related to noticing and shifting these small but powerful aspects of our practice. It is important to realize, however, that just as we can see multiple elements of the FAB framework in a single interaction, sometimes the same tool can be used in different ways, depending upon context. For instance, elongating a sound can provide emphasis to an important content word, which might help a teacher *be clear*, an element in **fostering an inviting environment**. The same practice—elongating a word to provide emphasis—can also be used to help mitigate teacher feedback that might otherwise sound punitive, another way of *fostering an inviting environment*, but in this case via *appreciating student mistakes*. Similarly, establishing mutual gaze can be another tool for *appreciating student mistakes*, but it can also be a way to **balance competing demands**, via *fostering equal participation*. In other words, not only do we see all three elements of the FAB framework working together, we see teachers using the same tools in different ways depending upon context. Above all, we believe that each classroom, each teacher, each student, and even each moment of classroom interaction is unique and, thus, worthy of our close attention and reflection. In fact, one of our main reasons for writing this book is to suggest that administrators and teacher-educators—and the assessments they use—need to take into account how incredibly complex and multifaceted teaching is. We discuss this complexity in more detail in Chapter 6.

Task 12

Think back to the transcripts we have looked at in Chapters 2–5. Make a list of the micro-tools teachers might use in creating a FAB environment. You might find it helpful to organize your list into two sections: verbal and non-verbal tools.

Chapter 6
Conclusion

To see a world in a grain of sand
And a heaven in a wild flower,
Hold infinity in the palm of your hand
And eternity in an hour.

—William Blake

Throughout this book, we have been intensely and repeatedly engaged in microscopic reflective work that zooms into the second-by-second transpiring of classroom interaction. We have, in other words, been gazing at William Blake's 'grain of sand' and 'wild flower.' In this final chapter, we wish to zoom out—by considering some of the larger themes and implications of this micro-reflective work. We wish to show, to the extent possible, the 'world' and the 'heaven' that can be seen through such micro-gazing. To that end, we revisit the FAB framework to highlight what lies beneath, and we argue that the micro-reflection we advocate constitutes an important step towards a micro-revolution (Creider, 2016) of classroom interaction.

THE FAB FRAMEWORK REVISITED

To the age-old saying *seeing is believing*, we add: *seeing is changing*. Our framework is based on the premise that one cannot change unless one sees—and sees the details of micro-moments. It follows that the kinds of reflection we are intent on cultivating are, unequivocally, micro. After all, teaching is the accumulation of micro-moments. There are undoubtedly myriad ways of conceptualizing such moments, and in this book, we have proposed one—in terms of FAB: foster an inviting environment, attend to learner voices, and balance competing demands. As should have become clear by now, our interest is in the unplanned nature of these moments, and more specifically, the contingencies and complexities of such unplanned moments. In other words, within the monumental enterprise called teaching, our reflective gaze has been exclusively calibrated to spotlight the part of teaching that must be built from one second to the next, given the specific individuals in the room with specific concerns at that specific moment on that specific day. Reflecting on such micro-moments of classroom interaction has been our preoccupation throughout this book.

To **foster an inviting environment**, for example, we note the various strategies that may be deployed to achieve being clear, being open, and being equal. Rather than prescribing clarity in broad terms, in other words, we draw attention to the specific conduct for achieving clarity such as **frame and focus** and **break it down**. More importantly, we show how these strategies are implemented in the micro-details of actual interaction through, for example, repeating key words or ideas and gesturing towards important places in the environment with precise timing. Similarly, attending to learner voice is not simply headlined as a slogan but demonstrated as an achievement brought off by skills such as providing contingent assistance and building on student talk. In order to provide contingent assistance, as we have shown, one can resort to strategies such as **offer before the 'ask'**, **adjust as it goes**, and **assist anyway**, and in the specifics of actual interaction, this can mean doing syllable-by-syllable micro-listening, using pauses, prosody, and gestures to give the gift of time, providing clues to narrow the field of possibilities, etc. Finally, balancing multiple demands entails balancing the agendas of the teacher and those of the students, and balancing the participation of individuals and the group. Teachers can balance agendas by, for example, **sharing the work** with the students using *let's*, using humor to **redirect** difficult student behavior, and **weaving** student language into their own talk by recycling that language word-for-word.

Much of what transpires in these micro-moments is about being responsive—to who the students are, what they have just said, and what is going on in the room at that very moment. We are being responsive when we provide contingent assistance and build on student talk for sure, but we are also being responsive when we strive for clarity in our instruction, allow for initiatives and blunders, and treat students as independent collaborators. In those cases, we are being responsive to students' needs to be seen and treated as competent. After all, confusion does not breed confidence, and nor does *not* having the freedom to explore or *not* being treated as someone who has valuable contributions to make. Finally, by balancing agendas and participation, we are being specifically responsive to the multiple demands that contingently arise in the stream of unfolding classroom interaction. In those cases, not being responsive would mean not seeing such multiplicity in the first place and attending to one concern at the expense of another.

So, to return to the question we posed earlier regarding CA's potential to change our reflective practices, what does all this have to do with reflection—or micro-reflection? The answer is: it offers a framework for what to reflect upon in the first place. As Farrell (2015) notes, 'reflecting on practice begins with an examination of our observable actions while we are teaching as well as our students' reactions (or non-reactions) during our lessons' (p. 29). However, when student teachers are asked to observe a class, they are often at a loss for what to look for. Looking for how corrective feedback is given with a set of predetermined categories, for example, is one way to go. We are proposing something different—by insisting on looking for what is happening in the raw materials of second-by-second interaction. By asking how learner voice is being attended to—syllable by syllable—by the participants themselves, we are not assuming the existence of corrective feedback *a priori*. Through such micro-gazing, we can become cognizant of how much more there is to be done with learner talk than merely correcting it. We get a sense of the most basic sense of 'micro' that is true to teacher and student concerns as they become evident in all the lively messiness of the classroom. We are, in other words, groping for a radical kind of 'micro.'

If the three components of FAB get at the 'micro' of micro-reflection, our cycle of noticing-changing constitutes the centerpiece of the 'reflection' in micro-reflection. It is our belief that the reflective cycle begins with noticing the various elements of FAB in their micro-details as laid out in the many examples throughout the book. This noticing is further cultivated during the 'change' phase where teachers are asked to engage in independent noticing or to 'see' on their own, to think on their own about the various decisions that can be made during a specific moment of classroom interaction, and to experiment on their own with these micro-decisions. Change is expected through such seeing, thinking, and experimenting, and ultimately, change should lead to further noticing. The cycle of micro-reflection continues, as shown in the figure in the first chapter, which we repeat here for convenience.

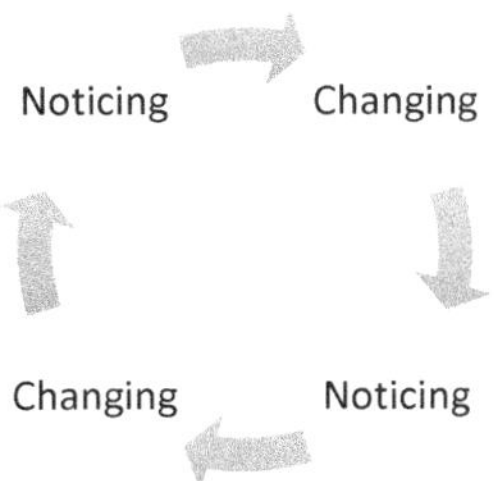

Figure The iterative cycle of micro-reflection

Our hope is that you can now start to fill in the arrows with actual teaching practices. For instance, you might decide that you want to focus on one element of the FAB framework, such as **Attend to learner voices**. If we return to that chapter, we can think about some of the moments we might notice, and some of the tools we might use for change:

Noticing => One student who always answers teacher questions.
Changing => Using *gaze* to acknowledge that student while verbally asking another question so someone else has a chance to talk or other changes you might think of.

Or, in case your focus is on **Balancing competing demands**:

Noticing => Pauses that might signal that a student is uncomfortable with a teacher suggestion.
Changing => Using *if* to offer a student a choice or other changes you might think of.

Clearly, we cannot stop after one round of noticing and changing. The reason that we talk about micro-reflection as a cycle, rather than a series of steps, is that once we try a new micro-tool, our next step is to notice what happens next! Maybe we are struggling with how to handle students who engage in side conversations with each other. As you may remember, this is a case of needing to **balance multiple demands.** We can start by noticing when this is occurring, and then, perhaps use humor as a way to gently redirect students, without seeming to be punitive or too controlling. But the cycle isn't complete yet. Once we have tried a new tool, we want to go back to noticing, to see how our students react. Maybe we realize that, in some contexts at least, humor is a tool that we want to keep using! Or maybe after some reflection, we notice that the reason students were talking to each other is that they didn't understand our directions. In that case, we may need to focus on being clear, which is an element of **fostering an inviting environment.**

Eventually, the 'micro' in 'micro-reflection' takes on a new meaning. Experienced teachers who are comfortable with lesson planning and with the content they are teaching, can move towards moments of reflection right in the middle of a conversation (cf. 'reflection-in-action' in Schön, 1983). As we are describing a game to a student, we might notice that their eyes are flickering from object to object. In that moment, we might decide to use a pointing gesture to help them find the important focus point in the game. That decision happens in a split second, but it makes the difference between a student who is confused and anxious and one who can focus on learning. We elucidate the power of such micro-reflection in the next section.

TOWARDS A MICRO-REVOLUTION IN CLASSROOM INTERACTION

Now that we have reviewed the FAB framework, we would like to spend some time discussing why we think the kind of reflection we describe in this book is so important. Like most people working in educational contexts today, we have moments of feeling overwhelmed. As a current bumper sticker reads: 'If you're not upset, you're not paying attention!' In other words, we are very aware of the big-picture issues facing our schools today. In no way do we wish to imply that micro-reflection can or should take the place of addressing the profound economic injustice faced by so many students today, or the racism, sexism, homophobia, and zenophobia that is rampant on a societal level—and, thus, apparent in our classrooms, hallways, lunchrooms, and schoolyards. At the same time, we also want to honor the moment-by-moment work so many teachers are accomplishing every day, and, hopefully, help to make that work even more powerful.

We use the word *power* advisedly, given that many teachers we know often feel power*less* in the face of standardized testing, increasing class sizes, and teacher assessments that feel punitive and unrelated to actual classroom realities. Like most teachers, we do not have the power to make the kinds of policy-level decisions that would change these issues. In fact, we believe that while policy is important, those of us who are interested in educational change also need to look at the detailed and complex world of teacher-student interactions. Even if teachers don't feel that they have agency within the walls of their classroom, they usually do have the power to effect change within the confines of their conversations. Whether we notice it or not, our choices regarding gesture, tone of voice, and language are impacting our students. If you take one thing away from this book, we hope it's an understanding of the power of noticing and using those micro-choices. To make this idea even more clear, we would like to look at three of the micro-resources we've discussed in Chapters 2–4, thinking about how they might have a macro-effect on classroom life.

The Power of Silence

We start with silence. In our experience, the most effective classrooms are spaces where there's a happy buzz of students engaging with each other and with the materials around them. What we are thinking of, then, is not the silence we hear teachers calling for in the hallway, or when they tell everyone to 'quiet down,' but rather the tiny moments of quiet that can occur between words, either while one person is talking, or right after one person finishes and before the next person starts. Researchers have found that people respond to even 6/10ths of a second of silence in conversation, which is why we are so careful to note such moments in our transcripts. As we noted at the end of Chapter 5, every context is different, which means that silence can have a variety of effects on our interactions. Here, we are going to look back at several different ways that a tiny moment of quiet can be a tool for empowering both teachers and students.

As we have discussed, silence can be used to set off the important word in a sentence, for instance, while a teacher is giving instructions. Being able to figure out what's important in a teacher's instructions can make the difference between a student who feels confused and anxious versus one who sees herself as focused and competent. Of course, students can use silence too. In fact, noticing silence in an interaction is one way teachers can figure out when their students need help. Letting a student sit miserably silent because they don't know what we're asking for is a recipe for an uninviting environment, one where students are too nervous to learn.

The Power of Saying 'Oh'

Unlike the multipurpose pause, *oh* is typically used in a specific context; when the speaker is showing that they have, just then, taken in new information (Heritage, 1984). Thus, when teachers preface a statement with 'oh,' they are showing that they have learned something, whether from the environment, or—better yet— from a student. As many researchers have noted, the teacher is generally seen as the 'primary knower' (Aukerman, 2007, p. 67) in the classroom, the one who has all the information. What happens, then, when the all-knowing teacher learns something new? Interestingly, when teachers act like learners, learners have the space to act like teachers, in the sense that they can suggest new topics, take responsibility for what happens next in the classroom, and speak with more authority (Creider, 2016). Such major shifts in student agency can begin with the simple use of *oh*.

The Power of Pointing

If we look at pointing closely, we note that it usually occurs in concert with other actions. A teacher who is skilled in the art of micro-noticing can take advantage of this fact. For instance, a common dilemma for teachers is trying to encourage quieter students without being rude to more talkative students. A solution might be to gesture to the student who is speaking, so that they know we are attending to them, while *looking* at the whole class—to make it clear that it's time for others to join in as well. In other words, something as instinctive and apparently minor as pointing can help teachers to handle one of the most difficult balancing acts of running a class.

As can be seen, these three teacher practices that last no more than a few seconds each can have major impact. We believe that they can be a first step along a path towards changing entrenched teacher-student dynamics, and towards building classrooms where student engagement is encouraged and student voices are welcomed. They are the sparks that will light the fire of micro-revolution.

Appendix A

Transcription Notations

.	(period) falling intonation
?	(question mark) rising intonation
,	(comma) continuing intonation
-	(dash) abrupt cut-off
::	(colon(s)) prolonging of sound
<u>w</u>ord	(underlining) stress
<u>wo</u>rd	the more underlining, the greater the stress
WORD	(all caps) loud speech
°word°	(degree symbols) quiet speech
↑word	(upward arrow) raised pitch
↓word	(downward arrow) lowered pitch
>word<	(more than and less than) quicker speech
<word>	(less than and more than) slowed speech
<	(less than) jump start or rushed start
hh	(series of h's) aspiration or laughter
.hh	(h's preceded by dot) inhalation
(hh)	(h's in parentheses) inside word boundaries
[ ]	(lined-up brackets) beginning and ending of simultaneous or overlapping speech or visual conduct
=	(equal sign) beginning of any next unit without a break
(2.4)	(number in parentheses) length of a silence in 10ths of a second
(.)	(period in parentheses) micro-pause, 0.2 second or less
( )	(empty parentheses) non-transcribable segment of talk

(comment)	transcriptionist comment
\$word\$	(dollar or pound signs) smiley voice
#word#	(number signs) creaky voice
word on numbered line	(italics) visual conduct <u>not</u> co-occurring with own talk (or silence)
word on unnumbered line	(italics) visual conduct co-occurring with own talk (or silence); applicable till end of turn unless otherwise noted
TC	teacher
ST	student
SS	students
TR	tutor
TT	tutee
MR	mentor
ME	mentee

Appendix B

List of Extracts

ceremony: p. 64
don't know if I can comment: p. 37
don't know if you're going to buy this: p. 58
eight: p. 30
endorphins: pp. 61, 62, 70
excellent: p. 33
expected ending: p. 98
gaze shift to class: p. 97
gossiping: p. 87
graduate and diploma: pp. 65, 66
green ones: p. 82
have seen: p. 69
help her forget: pp. 35, 36
homeless people: p. 43
how many eyes: p. 39
I go back and forth: p. 57
in a row: p. 86
Japanese humor: p. 108
let her talk: pp. 103, 104
make the story short: p. 32
mars and mardi: pp. 49, 50
melody: p. 109
missing in Alaska: pp. 40, 41
no questions: pp. 33, 43
number one: pp. 99, 100, 101
poetry: p. 55
polar bears: p. 55
pretty old: pp. 76, 77

produce: pp. 101, 102, 103
put you off your game: p. 52
red ones: pp. 89, 90
scholarship: pp. 63, 116, 117, 119, 120
silent butterflies: pp. 123, 125, 127
speed this up: p. 52
swallow: pp. 38, 45
the effect: pp. 71, 80
this is a car: p. 92
this one: p. 78
this side over here: p. 108
traditional drums: p. 111
upset: pp. 24, 25, 26
vocabulary review: p. 73
wanna share: p. 94
water: pp. 21, 22, 23
we wanna make four: p. 29
weekend: p. 74
what did they end in: p. 19
what do you do: p. 48
what is there to get: p. 106

References

Akbari, R. (2007). Reflections on reflection: A critical appraisal of reflective practices in L2 teacher education. *System*, 35, 192–207. https://doi.org/10.1016/j.system.2006.12.008

Antaki, C. (Ed.). (2011). *Applied conversation analysis: Intervention and change in institutional talk*. Basingstoke: Palgrave Macmillan. https://doi.org/10.1057/9780230316874

Atkinson, M. (2015). *Lend me your ears: All you need to know about making speeches and presentations*. Oxford: Oxford University Press.

Aukerman, M. S. (2007). When reading it wrong is getting it right: Shared evaluation pedagogy among struggling fifth graders. *Research in the Teaching of English*, 42(1), 56–102.

Barnes, D. (1976/1992). *From communication to curriculum*. Portsmouth, NH: Boynton/Cook-Heinemann.

Barron, B. (2006). Interest and self-sustained learning as catalysts of development: A learning ecology perspective. *Human Development*, 49, 193–224. https://doi.org/10.1159/000094368

Beauchamp, C. (2015). Reflection in teacher education: Issues emerging from a review of current literature. *Reflective Practice*, 16(1), 123–141. https://doi.org/10.1080/14623943.2014.982525

Boblett, N. (2018). Doing exploratory talk in the language classroom: A sequential account. *Haceteppe University Journal of Education*, 33, 261–277. https://doi.org/10.16986/HUJE.2018038806

Boblett, N. (2020). Working on understanding in the adult ESL classroom: A collaborative endeavor. Unpublished doctoral dissertation. Teachers College, Columbia University.

Bolden, G. (2006). Little words that matter: Discourse markers 'so' and 'oh' and the doing of other-attentiveness in social interaction. *Journal of Communication*, 56(4), 661–688. https://doi.org/10.1111/j.1460-2466.2006.00314.x

Brandt, C. (2008). Integrating feedback and reflection in teacher preparation. *ELT Journal*, 62(1), 37–46. https://doi.org/10.1093/elt/ccm076

Button, G. (1987). Moving out of closings. In Graham Button & John R. E. Lee (Eds.), *Talk and social organization* (pp. 101–151). Clevedon: Multilingual Matters.

Button, G. (1990). On varieties of closings. In George Psathas (Ed.), *Interactional competence* (pp. 93–148). Washington DC: International Institute of Ethnomethodology and Conversation Analysis and University Press of America.

Clayman, S., & Gill, V. (2004). Conversation analysis. In M. Hardy & A. Bryman (Eds.), *Handbook of data analysis* (pp. 589–606). Thousand Oaks, CA: Sage Publications.

Copland, F., Ma, G., & Mann, S. (2009). Reflecting in and on post-observation feedback in initial teacher training on certificate courses. *English Language Teacher Education and Development*, 12, 14–22.

Creider, S. (2012). 'One, two, one two': A teacher's use of speech, gesture, and the environment to impart information. *Language and Information Society*, 16, 43–78. https://doi.org/10.29211/soli.2012.16..003

Creider, S. (2013). The integration sequence: Responding to child initiations in a tutoring session. Unpublished manuscript. Teachers College, Columbia University.

Creider, S. (2014). Encouraging student participation in a French immersion kindergarten class: A multi-modal, conversation analytic study. Dissertation proposal, Teachers College, Columbia University.

Creider, S. (2016). Encouraging student participation in a French-immersion kindergarten class: A multimodal, conversation analytic study. Unpublished doctoral dissertation. Teachers College, Columbia. University.

Creider, S. C. (2020). Student talk as a resource: Integrating conflicting agendas in math tutoring sessions. *Linguistics and Education*, 58, 1–9.

Dewey, J. (1910). *How we think*. Boston: D. C. Heath & Co. https://doi.org/10.1037/10903-000

Drew, P., & Heritage, J. (Eds.). (1992). *Talk at work: Interaction in institutional settings.* Cambridge: Cambridge University Press.

Drew, P., Toerien, M., Irvine, A., & Sainsbury, R. (2014). Personal adviser interviews with benefits claimants in UK jobcentres. *Research on Language and Social Interaction*, 47(3), 306–316. https://doi.org/10.1080/08351813.2014.925669

Erickson, F. (1975). Gatekeeping and the melting pot: Interaction in counseling encounters. *Harvard Educational Review*, 45, 44–70. https://doi.org/10.17763/haer.45.1.g2x156r1k00w5037

Erickson, F. (2004). *Talk and social theory: Ecologies of speaking and listening in everyday life*. Cambridge, UK: Polity Press.

Fagan, D. S. (2012). Dealing with unexpected learner contributions in whole group activities: An examination of novice language teacher discursive practices. *Classroom Discourse*, 3(2), 107–128. https://doi.org/10.1080/19463014.2012.716621

Fagan, D. S. (2013). Managing learner contributions in the adult ESL classroom: A conversation analytic and ethnographic examination of teacher practices and cognition. Unpublished doctoral dissertation. Teachers College, Columbia University.

Fagan, D. S. (2015a). Managing language errors in real-time: A microanalysis of teacher practices. *System*, 55, 74–85. https://doi.org/10.1016/j.system.2015.09.004

Fagan, D. S. (2015b). When learner inquiries arise: Marking teacher cognition as it unfolds 'in-the-moment'. *Ilha do Desterro: A Journal of English Language, Literatures in English and Cultural Studies*, 68, 75–90. https://doi.org/10.5007/2175-8026.2015v68n1p75

Farrell, T. S. C. (2008). *Reflective language teaching: From research to practice*. London: Continuum Press.

Farrell, T. S. C. (2015). *Promoting teacher reflection in second language education: A framework for TESOL Professionals*. New York: Routledge. https://doi.org/10.4324/9781315775401

Farrell, T. S. C. (2018a). *Research on reflective practice in TESOL*. New York: Routledge. https://doi.org/10.4324/9781315206332

Farrell, T. S. C. (2018b). *Reflective language teaching: Practical applications for TESOL teachers*. London: Bloomsbury.

Farrell, T. S. C. (2019). *Reflective practice in ELT*. Bristol, CT: Equinox Publishing.

Gass, S., & Mackay, A. (2006). Input, interaction, and output. *AILA Review*, 19(3), 3–17. https://doi.org/10.1075/aila.19.03gas

Gladwell, M. (2000). *The tipping point: How little things make a big difference*. New York: Little Brown and Company.

Goodwin, C. (2013). The cooperative, transformative organization of human action and knowledge. *Journal of Pragmatics*, 46(1), 8–23. https://doi.org/10.1016/j.pragma.2012.09.003

Goodwin, C. (2018). *Co-operative action: Learning in doing*. Cambridge: Cambridge University Press.

Grushka, K., McLeod, J. H., & Reynolds, R. (2005). Reflecting upon reflection: Theory and practice in one Australian university teacher education program. *Reflective Practice*, 6(2), 239–246. https://doi.org/10.1080/14623940500106187

Hall, J. K. (2019). An EMCA approach to capturing the specialized work of L2 teaching: A research proposal. In M. Haneda & X. Nassaiji (Eds.), *Language as social action: Insights from socio-cultural perspectives* (pp. 228–245). Bristol: Multilingual Matters. https://doi.org/10.21832/9781788922944-017

Hansen, D. T. (2017). Bearing witness to teaching and teachers. *Journal of Curriculum Studies*, 49(1), 7–23. https://doi.org/10.1080/00220272.2016.1205137

Hatton, N., & Smith, D. (1995). Reflection in teacher education: Towards definition and implementation. *Teaching and Teacher Education*, 11(1), 33–49. https://doi.org/10.1016/0742-051X(94)00012-U

Hepburn, A., Wilkinson, S., & Butler, C. W. (2014). Intervening with conversation analysis in telephone helpline services: Strategies to improve effectiveness. *Research on Language and Social Interaction*, 47(3), 239–254. https://doi.org/10.1080/08351813.2014.925661

Heritage, J. (1984). A change of state token and aspects of its sequential placement. In J. Maxwell Atkinson & John Heritage (Eds.), *Structures of social action* (pp. 299–345). Cambridge, Cambridge University Press. https://doi.org/10.1017/CBO9780511665868.020

Heritage, J., & Clayman, S. (2010). *Talk in action: Interactions, identities, and institutions.* Malden, MA: Wiley-Blackwell. https://doi.org/10.1002/9781444318135

Heritage, J., & Robinson, J. D. (2011). 'Some' versus 'Any' medical issues: Encouraging patients to reveal their unmet concerns. In C. Antaki (Ed.), *Applied conversation analysis: Intervention and changes in institutional talk* (pp. 15–31). London: Palgrave Macmillan. https://doi.org/10.1057/9780230316874_2

Jacknick, C., & Creider, S. (2018). A chorus line: Engaging (or not) with the open floor. *Hacettepe University Journal of Education*, 33, 72–92. https://doi.org/10.16986/HUJE.2018038797

Jefferson, G. (1983). Notes on some orderliness of overlap onset. *Tilburg Papers in Language and Literature*, 28, 1–28.

Jefferson, G. (2004). Glossary of transcript symbols with an introduction. In G. Lerner (Ed.), *Conversation analysis: Studies from the first generation* (pp. 13–34). Amsterdam/Philadelphia: John Benjamins Publishing Company. https://doi.org/10.1075/pbns.125.02jef

Jenkins, L., & Reuber, M. (2014). A conversation analytic intervention to help neurologists identify diagnostically relevant linguistic features in seizure patients' talk. *Research on Language and Social Interaction*, 47(3), 266–279. https://doi.org/10.1080/08351813.2014.925664

Johnson, K. (1995). *Understanding communication in second language classrooms.* Cambridge: Cambridge University Press.

Johnson, K. E., & Dellagenlo, A. (2013). How 'sign meaning develops': Strategic mediation in learning to teach. *Language Teaching Research*, 17(4), 409–432. https://doi.org/10.1177/1362168813494126

Koshik, I. (2002). Designedly incomplete utterances: A pedagogical practice for eliciting knowledge displays in error correction sequences. *Research on Language and Social Interaction*, 35(3): 277–310.

Kunitz, S., Sert, O., & Markee, N. (Eds.) (forthcoming). *Emerging issues in classroom discourse and interaction.* New York: Springer.

Lawrence-Wilkes, L., & Ashmore, L. (2014). *The reflective practitioner in professional education.* New York: Palgrave Macmillan. https://doi.org/10.1057/9781137399595

Liu, K. (2015). Critical reflection as a framework for transformative learning in teacher education. *Educational Review*, 67(2), 135–157. https://doi.org/10.1080/00131911.2013.839546

Liu, K. (2017). Creating a dialogic space for prospective teacher critical reflection and transformative learning. *Reflective Practice*, 18(6), 805–820. https://doi.org/10.1080/14623943.2017.1361919

Long, M. H. (1983). Native speaker/non-native speaker conversation and the negotiation of comprehensible input. *Applied Linguistics*, 4, 126–141. https://doi.org/10.1093/applin/4.2.126

Luff, P., Patel, M., Kuzuoka, H., & Heath, C. (2014). Assembling collaboration: Informing the design of interaction spaces. *Research on Language and Social Interaction*, 47(3), 317–329. https://doi.org/10.1080/08351813.2014.925680

Lyster, R., Saito, K., & Sato, M. (2013). Oral corrective feedback in second language classrooms. *Language Teaching*, 46(1), 1–40. https://doi.org/10.1017/S0261444812000365

Markee, N. (2000). *Conversation analysis*. Mahwah, NJ: Laurence Erlbaum Associates. https://doi.org/10.4324/9781410606471

Mason, J. (2002). *Researching your own practice: The discipline of noticing*. London: Routledge Falmer. https://doi.org/10.4324/9780203471876

Maynard, D. W., Schaeffer, N. C., & Freese, J. (2011). Improving response rates in telephone interviews. In C. Antaki (Eds.), *Applied conversation analysis: Intervention and changes in institutional talk* (pp. 54–74). London: Palgrave Macmillan. https://doi.org/10.1057/9780230316874_4

McGarr, O., & Moody, J. (2010). Scaffolding or stifling? The influence of journal requirements on students' engagement in reflective practice. *Reflective Practice*, 11(5), 579–591. https://doi.org/10.1080/14623943.2010.516968

McHoul, A. W. (1985). Two aspects of classroom interaction: Turn-taking and correction. *Australian Journal of Human Communication Disorders*, 13(1), 53–64. https://doi.org/10.3109/asl2.1985.13.issue-1.04

Moll, L. C., Amanti, C., Neff, D., & Gonzalez, N. (1992). Funds of knowledge for teaching: Using a qualitative approach to connect homes and classrooms. *Theory into Practice*, 31(2), 132–141. https://doi.org/10.1080/00405849209543534

Morrell, E. (2002). Toward a critical pedagogy of popular culture: Literacy development among urban youth. *Journal of Adolescent & Adult Literacy*, 46(1), 72–77.

Psathas, G. (1995). *Conversation analysis: The study of talk-in-interaction*. Thousand Oaks, CA: Sage. https://doi.org/10.4135/9781412983792

Reddington, E. (2018). Managing participation in the adult ESL classroom: Engagement and exit practices. *Classroom Discourse*, 9(2), 132–149. https://doi.org/10.1080/19463014.2018.1433051

Rodgers, C. (2002). Defining reflection: Another look at John Dewey and reflective thinking. *Teachers College Record*, 104(4), 842–866. https://doi.org/10.1111/1467-9620.00181

Rodgers, C. (2006). Attending to student voice: The impact of descriptive feedback on learning and teaching. *Curriculum Inquiry*, 36(2), 209–237.

Saito, E., & Khong, T. D. H. (2017). Not just for special occasions: Supporting the professional learning of teachers through critical reflection with audio-visual information. *Reflective Practice*, 18(6), 837–851. https://doi.org/10.1080/14623943.2017.1361921

Salaberry, M. R., & Kunitz, S. (Eds.) (2019), *Teaching and testing L2 interactional competence: Bridging theory and practice*. New York: Routledge. https://doi.org/10.4324/9781315177021

Schegloff, E. A. (1982). Discourse as an interactional achievement: Some uses of 'uh huh' and other things that come between sentences. In Deborah Tannen (Ed.), *Analyzing discourse: Text and talk* (pp. 71–93). Washington DC: Georgetown University Press.

Schegloff, E. A., & Sacks, H. (1973). Opening up closings. *Semiotica*, 7, 289–327. https://doi.org/10.1515/semi.1973.8.4.289

Schön, D. A. (1983). *The reflective practitioner: How professionals think in action*. New York: Basic Books.

Seedhouse, P. (2004). *The interactional architecture of the language classroom: A conversation analysis perspective*. Malden, MA: Blackwell.

Seedhouse, P. (2008). Learning to talk the talk: Conversation analysis as a tool for induction of trainee teachers. In S. Garten & K. Richards (Eds.), *Professional encounters in TESOL: Discourses of teachers in teaching* (pp. 42–57). New York, NY: Palgrave Macmillan. https://doi.org/10.1057/9780230594173_3

Sert, O. (2015). *Social interaction and L2 classroom discourse*. Edinburgh: Edinburgh University Press.

Sikveland, R. O., & Stokoe, E. (2016). Dealing with resistance in initial intake and inquiry calls to mediation: The power of 'willing'. *Conflict Resolution Quarterly*, 33(3), 235–253. https://doi.org/10.1002/crq.21157

Sinclair, J. M., & Coulthard, M. (1975). *Towards an analysis of discourse: The English used by teachers and pupils*. London: Oxford University Press.

Sparks-Langer, G. M., Simmons, J. M., Pasch, M., Colton, A., & Starko, A. (1990). Reflective pedagogical thinking: How can we promote it and measure it? *Journal of Teacher Education*, 41(4), 23–32. https://doi.org/10.1177/002248719004100504

Stivers, T. (2004). 'No no no' and other types of multiple sayings in social interaction. *Human Communication Research*, 30, 260–293. https://doi.org/10.1111/j.1468-2958.2004.tb00733.x

Stokoe, E. (2014). The Conversation-Analytic Role-Play Method (CARM): A method for training communication skills as an alternative to simulated role-play. *Research on Language and Social Interaction*, 47, 255–265. https://doi.org/10.1080/08351813.2014.925663

Swain, M. (1985). Communicative competence: Some roles of comprehensible input and comprehensible output in its development. In S. Gass & C. Madden (Eds.), *Input in second language acquisition* (pp. 235–253). Rowley, MA: Newbury House.

Tadic, N. (2019). 'My brain hurts:' Incorporating learner interests into the classroom. *Language and Education*, 33(1), 68–84. https://doi.org/10.1080/09500782.2018.1476527

van Lier, L. (1996). *Interaction in the language curriculum*. London: Longman Group Limited.

Vygotsky, L. S. (1978). *Mind in society: The development of higher psychological processes*. Cambridge, MA: Harvard University Press.

Walsh, S. (2006). *Investigating classroom discourse*. New York: Routledge. https://doi.org/10.4324/9780203015711

Walsh, S. (2011). *Exploring classroom discourse: Language in action*. New York: Routledge. https://doi.org/10.4324/9780203827826

Walsh, S., & Mann, S. (2015). Doing reflective practice: A data-led way forward. *ELT Journal*, 69(4), 351–362. https://doi.org/10.1093/elt/ccv018

Waring, H. Z. (2008). Using explicit positive assessment in the language classroom: IRF, feedback, and learning opportunities. *The Modern Language Journal*, 92(4), 577–594. https://doi.org/10.1111/j.1540-4781.2008.00788.x

Waring, H. Z. (2009). Moving out of IRF (initiation-response-feedback): A single case analysis. *Language Learning*, 59, 796–824. https://doi.org/10.1111/j.1467-9922.2009.00526.x

Waring, H. Z. (2011). Learner initiatives and learning opportunities. *Classroom Discourse*, 2(2), 201–218. https://doi.org/10.1080/19463014.2011.614053

Waring, H. Z. (2012). 'Any questions?': Investigating understanding-checks in the language classroom. *TESOL Quarterly*, 46(4), 722–752. https://doi.org/10.1002/tesq.48

Waring, H. Z. (2013). Managing Stacy: A case study of turn-taking in the language classroom. *System*, 41(3), 841–851. https://doi.org/10.1016/j.system.2013.08.007

Waring, H. Z. (2014). Turn allocation and context: Broadening participation in the second language classroom. In J. Flowerdew (Ed.), *Discourse in context: Contemporary applied linguistics Volume 3* (pp. 301–320). London: Bloomsbury Publishing.

Waring, H. Z. (2015). Promoting self-discovery in the language classroom. *International Review of Applied Linguistics in Language Teaching (IRAL)*, 53(1), 61–85. https://doi.org/10.1515/iral-2015-0003

Waring, H. Z. (2016). *Theorizing pedagogical interaction: Insights from conversation analysis*. New York: Routledge. https://doi.org/10.4324/9781315751351

Waring, H. Z. (2019). The what and how of English language teaching: Conversation analytic perspectives. In X. Gao (Ed.), *Second handbook of English language teaching* (pp. 1053–1070). New York: Springer, Cham.

Waring, H. Z. (forthcoming). Harnessing the power of heteroglossia in teacher talk. In S. Kunitz, O. Sert, & N. Markee (Eds.), *Emerging issues in classroom discourse and interaction*. New York: Springer.

Waring, H. Z., & Carpenter, L. (2019). Gaze shifts as a resource for managing attention and participation. In J. K. Hall & S. Looney (Eds.), *The embodied work of teaching* (pp. 122–141). Clevedon: Multilingual Matters.

Waring, H. Z., & Hruska, B. (2012). Problematic directives in pedagogical interaction. *Linguistics and Education*, 23, 289–300. https://doi.org/10.1016/j.linged.2012.06.002

Waring, H. Z., Reddington, E., & Tadic, N. (2016). Responding artfully to student-initiated departures in the adult ESL classroom. *Linguistics and Education*, 33, 28–39. https://doi.org/10.1016/j.linged.2015.12.001

Waring, H. Z., & Yu, D. (2016). Life outside the classroom as a resource for language learning. *Language Learning Journal*. https://doi.org/10.1080/09571736.2016.1172332

Wilkinson, S. (2011). Changing interactional behavior: Using conversation analysis in intervention programmes for aphasic conversation. In C. Antaki (Eds.), *Applied conversation analysis: Intervention and changes in institutional talk* (pp. 32–53). London: Palgrave Macmillan. https://doi.org/10.1057/9780230316874_3

Index

adjust as it goes 63–65, 132
Akbari, R. 2
Antaki, C. 7
appreciate student mistakes 40–41
Ashmore, L. 3
assist anyway 63, 65–67, 132
Atkinson, M. 7
attend to learner voices 11, 60–83, 131–134
Aukerman, M. S. 136

balance competing demands 10, 84–110, 129, 131–134
balancing agendas 85–86
balancing participation 96–105
Barnes, D. 34
Barron, B. 60
Beauchamp, C. 2–3
being clear 28–31, 132
being equal 47–54, 132
being open 31–47, 132
Boblett, N. 24–26, 34–36, 38
Bolden, G. 50, 136
Brandt, C. 2
break it down 24–28, 132
building on student talk 72–79, 132
Butler, C. W. 5, 7
Button, G. 114

Carpenter, L. 36, 97
choice points 8
Clayman, S. 6–7
conversation analysis (CA) 6–9
Copland, F. 2

Coulthard, M. 32
Creider, S. 4, 6, 21–23, 29–30, 39, 49–50, 55, 73, 75–78, 82, 85–86, 89–90, 92, 122–123, 127, 131, 136

Dellagenlo, A. 11, 60
develop 74–76
Dewey, J. 1–3
Drew, P. 7

embroider 76–79, 132
engage in exploratory talk 34–37
Erickson, F. 51, 98
evidence-based teacher training 9

Fagan, D. S. 34, 36, 40, 41, 71, 80
Farrell, T. S. C. 2–5, 83, 129, 133
fostering an inviting environment 11, 18–59, 132–134
Freese, J. 7

Gass, S. 18
Gill, V. 6
Gladwell, M. 8
Goodwin, C. 60, 113
Grushka, K. 3

Hall, J. K. 8, 9
Hansen, D. T. 4, 11
Hatton, N. 3
Hepburn, A. 5, 7, 8, 76
Heritage, J. 6, 7, 51
Hruska, B. 19–20

initiation-response-feedback (IRF) 32

Jacknick, C. 4, 73
Jefferson, G. 6, 113
Jenkins, L. 7
Johnson, K. 11, 20, 60

Khong, T. D. H. 3
Koshik, I. 20
Kunitz, S. 8

Lawrence-Wilkes, L. 3

Moody, J. 2
Morrell, E. 60

offer before the 'ask' 60–64, 132

package of teachers' exiting practices 112
participation paradox 96
position others as independent agent 51–53
position self as learner 48–51
provide frame and focus 21–24, 132
providing contingent assistance 60–72
Psathas, G. 4

Reddington, E. 87, 94, 96, 109, 111–112,
     114
redirect humorously 87–88, 132–134
reflection, reflective practice 1–6
     five stages/levels 3
     noticing-changing 5–6, 134
     reflection-in-action 134
Reuber, M. 7
Reynolds, R. 3
Robinson, J. D. 7
Rodgers, C. 2, 5

Sacks, H. 6–7
Saito, E. 3
Saito, K. 40
Salaberry, M. R. 8

Sato, M. 40
Schaeffer, N. C. 7
Schegloff, E. A. 6–7, 113
Schön, D. A. 1–3, 134
Seedhouse, P. 8, 20
Sert, O. 8, 10, 16
share the work 86–87
shifting focus from the 'eager' individual
     97–101
Sikveland, R. O. 7
Sinclair, J. M. 32
Smith, D. 3
Sparks-Langer, G. M. 3
Stivers, T. 114
Stokoe, E. 7, 8
student-centered and interest-driven
     pedagogy 60
Swain, M. 18
symmetry 47

Tadic, N. 60, 87, 94
three principles of pedagogical interaction
     10
     competence 10
     complexity 10
     contingency 10
transcription 6, 138–139
turn shark 98

van Lier, L. 47, 60
Vygotsky, L. S. 60

Walsh, S. 2–5, 8
Waring, H. Z. 6, 8, 12–15, 19, 20, 32, 33,
     36, 37, 43, 48, 52, 55, 57, 58, 60, 61, 62,
     64, 69, 70, 74, 84, 85, 87, 94, 97–104,
     106, 108
weave 88–91, 132
welcome student initiations 37–39
Wilkinson, S. 5, 7

Yu, D. 60

CPSIA information can be obtained
at www.ICGtesting.com
Printed in the USA
JSHW020218170321
12546JS00002B/2